BOOKBINDING BASICS

To Gianna with deepest gratitude
To Rita for her acknowledgement of me
To my grandfather, Dario, who was a straw craftsman

Many thanks to the friends and relatives who helped me in the making of this book:
Piero and Marcella Dallai of Florence—master bookbinders—for their advice, hospitality, and generosity, and for making the sewing frame and press photographed in this book available to me
Lea Bilanci, a true artist with paper and books for having "saved" me on various occasions, and for letting me have the vegetable paper that appears in this book
Francesca and Giulia Mannori, Paola Ballerini, and Gianni Cascone for having entrusted me with the signatures and encyclopaedias for binding
Ilaria and Roberta Pugi for *Astronomia*, a book very dear to them
Gianni Rosati for helping me in planning new equipment
Vanessa Colivicchi for the designs
Sara, Daniela, Sonia, Aldo, and Ada Rosati for being there
Maria Chiara Bettini and Alessandro Bertini for the last e-mails
Lucia, Emma, and Franco for sun-filled afternoons

The Firms that made indispensable materials available:
Miliani Fabriano, in particular Mr. Guasti and the extremely kind Miss Gianna in the Commercial Office, for the precious paper and sets of samples
Giardini, Milan, to the most kind Mr. Capasso and Mr. Ciappello, for having obtained papers, headbands, and cloths for me
Mr. Marco Magheri of the Falegnameria M.B.S. Service of Poggio a Caiano (Prato), for making the sewing frame and the two hand presses
Mr. Giorgio of the Tipografia Azzurra of Seano (Carmignano), Prato
Mesticheria Giacomelli of Prato
Renkalik of Bologna

Heartfelt thanks to Cristina Sperandeo, Paola Masera, Beatrice Brancaccio, Laura Casnici, Bruno Balzano, and Alberto Bertoldi.

Editor: Cristina Sperandeo
Photography: Alberto Bertoldi
Translation: Chiara Tarsia
Graphic design and layout: Paola Masera with Beatrice Brancaccio

Library of Congress Cataloging-in-Publication Data Available

10   9   8   7   6   5   4   3   2   1

Published in 2001 by Sterling Publishing Co., Inc.
387 Park Avenue South, New York, NY 10016

Originally published in Italy under the title *Rilegatura: Tecnica, Idee, Progetti* by RCS Libri S.p.A.
via Mecenate, 91, 20138 Milan

© 1998 RCS Libri S.p.A., Milano
I Edizione Grandi Manuali Fabbri ottobre 1998
English Translation © 2001 by Sterling Publishing
Distributed in Canada by Sterling Publishing
c/o Canadian Manda Group, One Atlantic Avenue, Suite 105
Toronto, Ontario, M6K 3E7, Canada
Distributed in Great Britain and Europe by Cassell PLC
Wellington House, 125 Strand, London, WC2R 0BB, England
Distributed in Australia by Capricorn Link (Australia) Pty Ltd.
P.O. Box 704, Windsor, NSW 2756, Australia

Printed in China

Sterling ISBN 0-8069-7939-9

Paola Rosati

BOOKBINDING
BASICS

Sterling Publishing Co., Inc.
New York

CONTENTS

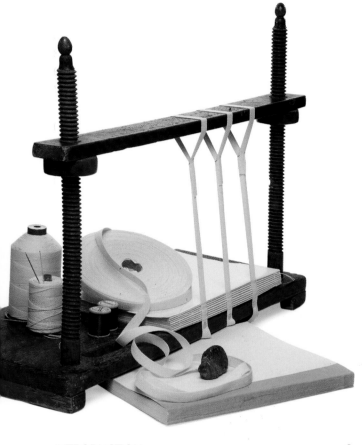

Papers 28
SEWING WITH A SEWING FRAME 30
The Sewing Frame. 30
The Book Press 30
Other Materials for Sewing with a Sewing Frame 32
Various Tools and Accessories 34

BASIC RULES 37

The Grain of the Cardboard 38
The Grain of the Paper. 38
Aligning the Paper. 39
Counting the Sheets. 40
Counting Fanned Sheets 41
Folding the Sheets. 42
Glue 43
Natural Adhesives 43
Synthetic Adhesives 43
Direct Gluing 43
Ribbon Gluing. 43
SEWING 44
Sawing. 44
Link-Stitch Sewing 44
Half-Stitch Sewing 45
Full-Stitch Sewing. 45
Flyleaves 46
Glued Flyleaves 46
German-style Folded Flyleaves 46

INTRODUCTION. 6

A BRIEF HISTORICAL OUTLINE 8
GLOSSARY. 12

MATERIALS 15

CARDBOARD 16
PAPER 18
Machine Made Paper. 18
Special Characteristics. 18
Paper for Inside Pages. 20
Paper for Flyleaves. 22
Industrial Paper for Covers 24
Handmade Paper 26
Painted Paper 26
CLOTH AND PAPERS. 28
Cloth for Covers 28

PROJECTS 49

HALF CLOTH AND PAPER JOURNAL. 50
Requirements 52
Preparations for Sewing. 53
Aligning the Sheets. 54
Counting and Folding the Sections. 56
Sawing. 58

Glued Flyleaves 60
Sewing. 62
Preparing the Sewing Frame 63
Sewing. 64
Making the Book Block. 69
Tightening the Twines 70
Gluing 71
The Case Cover with Cloth Corners 75
Measuring the Cover 76
Cutting the Cardboard 76
Cutting the Cloth 77
Cutting the Paper. 78
Gluing the Cloth. 79
Gluing the Paper 82
Positioning the Book Block 85
Casing. 86

HALF CLOTH AND PAPER JOURNAL
WITH A ROUNDED SPINE 88
Requirements 90
Preparing for Sewing. 91
Aligning the Sheets. 92
Counting the Sections 92
Double Flyleaves 93
Sawing. 95
Sewing. 96
Making the Book Block. 98
Tightening the Twines 99
Gluing 99

Rounding 100
Case Cover 102
Rounding the Spine 104

BINDING PUBLICATIONS INTO A BOOK. 106
Requirements 108
Sewing 109
The Cloth Cover 117

BINDING BY SEWING ON TAPE. 120
Requirements 122
Sewing with Tape 123
Making the Cover 128

BINDING A NOTEBOOK ON A HOMEMADE
SEWING FRAME 132
Requirements 134
From Sewing to the Cover 135

BINDING WITHOUT A SEWING FRAME 141

BINDING WITH NAILS 142
Requirements 144
From Aligning to the Cover. 145

A SEWN NOTEBOOK. 152
Requirements 154
From Folding to the Sewn Notebook 155

INDEX 160

INTRODUCTION

A long time ago I had a dream. I was going into the printing works where I had worked for years. There wasn't the usual neon lighting. The whole building was illuminated with sunlight: the machines, the work desks, and the paper were all were lit up by unusual beams of light...

Normally, it is the white of the paper that always overpowers the other shades of color. But now, instead, there were warm and soft colors. It was as if everything was all packed together in an orange-colored tone, which flooded everything with light. But this "everything" wasn't the books, or brushes, or paper, or even the printing machines. No, everything had become a great orchard and vegetable garden—fresh vegetables, bathed with the morning dew; fruits of all seasons were neatly in line and ready to be printed in place of the paper, which was waiting to be headed; the paper sheets; the brushes with glue; the cloth; and the mull.

I gazed, amazed and incredulous. I slipped on my overalls and strolled in this fantastic garden that was so strangely silent (in the printing works, as you know, silence is impossible). Oranges, lettuce, cabbage leaves, peaches, and tomatoes were arranged on wooden shelves that reached to the ceiling.

And silence again accompanied me as I wandered between the benches and baskets of that unusual and unexpected market.

When I awoke I could think of nothing that had happened that could be linked to this dream. At that time I had already left the printing works and had been teaching for many years.

I have described this dream because it was those colors and those images that guided me in the planning of this book.

My first idea was to combine technical suggestions with "open book" projects, paying special attention to not only sewing, which is a key aspect of technique, but also to all those preliminary and essential operations such as aligning, counting, and folding paper.

Bookbinding means, first of all, knowing how to handle paper and getting the correct "hang" of the book. Gaining confidence in these operations means being able to start off in the proper way and to learn what technique really is.

Do not be afraid of by the new terms and the difficult, precise steps because these techniques, once acquired, will enable you to express your creative skills to the fullest, an element that is a technique in itself.

I don't know whether I've succeeded in my intention of introducing you to this ancient craft by persuading you to bind your own books, but I hope that those of you who, like me, love paper and books in their entirety, may stroll and wander through the pages in this book with wonder and curiosity as if you were in a great open-market.

Bookbinding can be done!

Paola Rosati

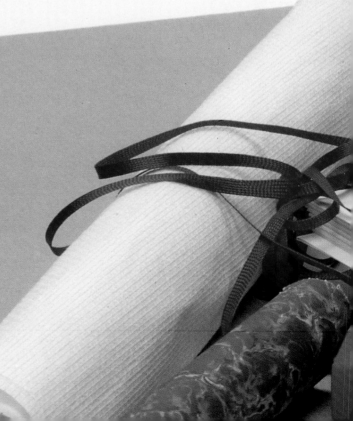

A BRIEF HISTORICAL OUTLINE

Binding means to make, fasten, or secure (bind in Latin is *ligare,* and *lygein* in Greek, means to knot). The Greek word, *lygos* (wickerwork) stems from the Sanskrit *ling-âmi,* which means "to fold or to embrace"; so, the etymological connections are evident. In our case, bookbinding stands for securing one sheet or folio, a term used for writing paper, with a thread. Continuing our journey into the meaning and connection of words, we come to the Latin word *folium,* which means "a leaf", like the leaf of a tree. The Latin word for book, *liber,* means "the bark or rind of a tree."

Book (liber), therefore, is the innermost part of the three strata making up the bark of a tree: rind, sapwood, and bark—the surface on which our ancestors mainly wrote. From this use came the word "book," understood as any material containing writing.

The first materials used to carve writing on were clay, stone, wood, bronze, and papyrus, which is the inner part of the tree (from 3,000 to 200 BCE). The first tablets, called "codex", were fastened together with hinges, rings, or ox gut, and folded over to form a diptych, triptych, or polyptych (from the Greek word *diptychos* meaning "folded twice").

This type of "book" was in opposition to the "volume" that the Egyptians made with papyrus bands. The sheets were rolled up and the bands of papyrus were glued together around a stiff roller, forming the scroll. The papyrus bands were written on in narrow parallel columns called *paginae* (from the Latin *pango,* "to write") that indicated the written sheets. When papyrus exportation fell heavily, new methods were invented for treating animal skins. This new material obtained, parchment (which gets its name from the city of Pergamum from where it initially was first made), soon substituted papyrus and eventually ousted it completely. The surface of parchment was smoother and presented advantages such as greater toughness, flexibility, and the possibility of reusing it. In fact, it could even be written on again when scraped.

The parchment bands, at first tied in volumes, were soon bound in codex form. However, we are still far from being able to say that binding had become established since it had not developed according to specific criteria. We must await the Middle Ages before binding can be considered as "clothing" or written sheets. With the fall of the Roman Empire, a whole civilization was dissolving. The need to preserve its memory through the written word stimulated research on the part of those who held works judged worthy to be handed down and preserved.

This is the case of the *monaci ligatores,* the "monk binders of books" who, during the Middle Ages, developed this craft in their monasteries and created real masterpieces by covering the sheets by fastening them together with wooden boards covered in inlaid ivory and then embroidering silk and precious stones onto them. The sacred writings of this period give vivid testimony of this.

In the monasteries, the art of bookbinding grew more and more refined. With the invention of printing press in the 15th century by Gutenberg, the document and bookmaking scenario changed completely. The bookbinding craftsmen were ready to develop new techniques that were better suited for volumes made in a new manner. Hemp cords substituted ox gut while heavy wooden boards gave way to

pasteboards, to which the first page (the frontispiece or title page) was glued on as a flyleaf.

This was a considerable step forward. The ease of handling books together with protection (insects are less fond of paper than of wood) now seemed assured, or almost. By the 16th century the form of the book and the binding techniques had become definitive. During the course of the following centuries only people's taste and their sensibility towards books were to change.

BOOKBINDING: AN EXPRESSION OF AN ERA

The history of bookbinding developed along with the evolution of furnishing styles. Important bookbinding centers sprang up all over Europe. Gradually, religiously inspired decorations were abandoned in favor of lay emblems and regal symbols. This is the era of the great master printers: in Venice, Aldo Manuzio invented a new type of punch for reproducing book decorations and—encouraged by the famous French bibliophile, Grolier, and the Milanese Masoli—went on to create new motifs for his bindings. Manuzio, Grolier, and Masoli were the trio who gave new impetus to the book making craft in Europe. The Court bookbinders worked under the protection of their art patrons, and often the covers of a book became true masterpieces. An example is the cover in gold and precious stones by Benvenuto Cellini commissioned by Cardinal Dei Medici, who presented it to the Emperor Charles V. Other famous names of the craft in France are the Clovis brothers, Nicolas Eve, and "le Gascon", whose real name is unknown. In England the great names were Reynes and Berthelet. Louis XIV, a monarch whose reign was extremely long and who was a patron of all the arts, upon ascending the throne made his mark also on the art of bookbinding. The style became even more precious, often too ornate, complicated, and laden with gold.

Madame de Pompadour gathered around her the artistic flower of her time and left her imprint on everything, from beautiful bookbinding (though very ornate and laden with gold) to a whole series of small objects in leather: cases, caskets, telescope handles, and sword sheaths.

The Pompadour style has curves covered in twisted leaves, clusters of flowers, cherubim, and birds.

After Louis XVI other sovereigns, princes, and ordinary people—guided by their love of books—went on to enrich the art of bookbinding and to adapt it to the style of the times.

For a long time innovations were mainly concerned with the techniques and the decorative motifs, and it could be said that the history of bookbinding is essentially a history of ornamental styles.

Alongside the ancient intaglio decoration on leather, the blind printing technique (without the use of gold) became popular (this would eventually oust the intaglio style completely). This type of decoration was very common in the 15th century and up to the middle of the 16th century. Gilding with heated tools and gold leaf, an imitation of the ancient process that the Arabs used, began to dominate bookbinding. This technique has been handed down and is still used today by master bookbinders in leather.

The 17th and 18th century decorations begin to take on different characteristics according to the tastes of the various periods and countries. Craftsmen-artists were able to express their individual styles as they pleased.

From this moment on production began to diversify: on one hand the precious materials intended for aristocrats and wealthy bibliophiles were enriched with artistic bindings while on the other the production of commercial bindings began and already contained a hint of future mass production. For economic reasons even the material itself began to be used sparingly, or worked so as to be usable even if shoddy or defective. This is the reason why leather started to be marbled in the 17th century, as an expedient to cover up defects. In the 18th century the use of leather for the spine was only tested, which led to the half-cloth binding that was to dominate the 19th century.

Influenced by radical social changes and the increase in the demand for books, techniques were adopted to meet this demand.

It was during this period that the technique of sewn sunken cords, instead of cords protruding along the spine, was invented: it was a Greek style imitation of the medieval bindings in the Byzantine East. In 1775, Alexis-Pierre Bradel created the separate cover in cloth and paper, similar to a file, into which the book block could be cased and glued to the first page.

On the threshold of the 20th century a new decorative technique called "symbolic" or "speaking" made its appearance on the scene, breaking with tradition. From then on decoration and the type of binding could never again be separated from the contents and the spirit of the book.

GLOSSARY

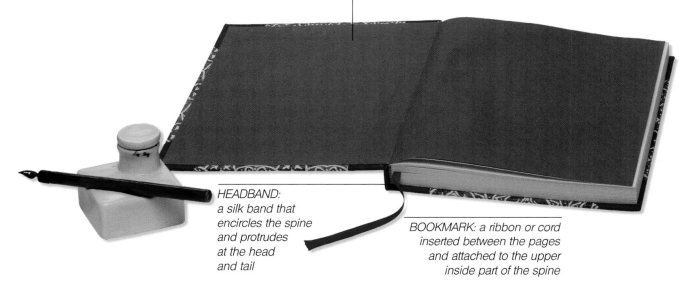

FLYLEAVES: situated at the beginning and end of a book; the leaves are folded in two parts, one of which is pasted to the inside of the cover while the other forms the first or last page

HEADBAND: a silk band that encircles the spine and protrudes at the head and tail

BOOKMARK: a ribbon or cord inserted between the pages and attached to the upper inside part of the spine

BACK: the side of the signatures along which the leaves are folded; a synonym for spine

BACKING: a light-weight strip of cardboard that is placed between the spine and the covering to stiffen the latter

BACKLINING: a stiff strip that acts as the base for making the spine; it is made of the same material as the cover

BANDS: the sewing supports (cords) when they are not sunk, but are outside the spine

BINDING: all the operations used in making a book by sewing the signatures to the spine

BOARDS: the cover boards when they are made of wood

BOOK BLOCK: all of the sheets making up the book; understood as an entity independent of the cover

BOOKMARK: a ribbon or cord inserted between the pages and attached to the upper-inside part of the spine

BRIEF DRYING: bookbinding jargon which means a very short drying time once the glue is spread on

CASING: the operation in which the book block is inserted and joined to the cover by pasting the flyleaves

COLOPHON: also called

publisher's postcript, it is, in a printed book, the final annotation which gives the printer's name, location, and date of publication

CORNERS: the covering for the corners of the cover boards in half-cloth binding; it is made of the same material that is used for covering the spine and the shoulders

COVER BOARDS: the two side parts of the cover that cover the surfaces of the book; also the cardboard pieces before they are covered

COVER: the structure or material that covers the book block

COVERING: the material

which covers the cover structure; also the operation of applying it

CREASING: the groove, which in bookbinding is made with a particular machine or manually with a bone folder, that folds paper and cardboard without damaging them

EDGE: the three-side surfaces along which the book opens; corresponds to the outer borders of the sheets

FLAPS: the cover board turn-ins of typographic covers

FLYLEAVES: situated at the beginning and the end of a book; the leaves are folded in two parts, one of which is

EDGE: the three side surfaces along which the book opens; corresponds to the outer borders of the sheets

COVER BOARDS: the two side parts of the cover that cover the surfaces of the book; also the cardboard pieces before they are covered

SPINE: the side of the book along which the signatures are sewed together

HEAD: the upper part of the book

SIGNATURE OR SECTION: two or more sheets folded in half and inserted into each other; the result of folding the printed or blank sheets

COVER: the structure of any type or material that covers the book

TAIL: the lower part of the book

pasted to the inside of the cover while the other forms the first and last pages of the book

FORE-EDGE: in books with rounded spines, this is the rounded recess along the whole edge of the book

GAP: a small space left between the shoulder and the tip of the cover boards so that they can open more easily

GROOVE: the groove between the spine and the board covers

HEAD: the upper part of the book

HEADBAND: the silk band that encircles the spine and protrudes at the head and tail

ROUNDING: the operation involved in making the spine rounded

SCRUBBING BRUSH: a horsehair or plastic brush, normally used for washing, that is good for making materials (paper and mull) stick

SEWING: the operation that enables the signatures to be kept together; it can be done in link-stitch, half-stitch, or full-stitch

SHOULDER: obtained by rounding; it is the same thickness as the cover boards

SIGNATURE or SECTION: two or more sheets folded in half and inserted into each other; the

result of folding the printed or blank sheets

SPINE: the side of the book in which the signatures are sewed together

SPLIT NUTS: the wooden nuts placed under the head beam of the sewing frame; they are used to pull the cords and tapes taut

SQUARE (PROJECTING EDGE): slight protrusion of the cover boards beyond the page edges for protection purposes

SURFACES: the front and back surfaces of the book

TAIL: lower part of the book

TAPPING (ALIGNING): a recurring operation that is necessary for keeping the

edges of the sheets and the backs of the signatures aligned

TITLE PAGE: the page that proceeds the text and bears the title and author's name

TRIMMING: carried out on individual signatures to even them out and make them the same size

TURN-INS: strips of the covering material that are folded in and pasted onto the borders of the reverse side of the cover boards and the two ends of the backing

WASTE PAPER: a technical term to define all the paper (newspaper and wrapping paper) that are used as a support while working

MATERIALS

Bookbinding uses various materials. Although a more in-depth knowledge comes with experience, it is a good idea to at least have a look at the most essential materials. Some research about the types and uses of paper, cardboard, and cloth could be of great help when approaching and trying out bookbinding techniques.

CARDBOARD

grey board $^1/_8$ inch

This is a product of the paper industry that is stiffer, thicker, and heavier than paper.

The manufacturing processes and the raw materials used are no different from those employed for paper, but the raw materials used are of poorer quality. The names of the various types of cardboard actually come from the glues that are used to make it.

GREY BOARD: is obtained from recycled paper; it is not high quality, but is sturdy.

MILL BOARD is heavy, smooth, strong, and stiff.

BRISTOL contains rag paste, and is named this because it was once made in Bristol, England. It is compact, layered, very heavy, and is available in glazed and semi-glossy surfaces.

STRAW BOARD is yellow and rough. It is rarely used.

MACHINE MADE is white, porous, and much more fragile than the previous types of cardboard.

The cardboards that are mostly used in bookbinding (employed for making covers) are grey board and mill board because of their compactness, sturdiness, and durability. The other types can be used as accessories during work. Regarding thickness, the $^1/_8$ inch and the $^1/_{16}$ inch are used when cutting rectangles for the cover; the $^1/_{32}$ inch is used for the spine when rounded-spine day planners or books are involved. Other common thicknesses are the $^3/_{32}$ inch and the $^1/_{32}$ inch. For cutting $^1/_8$-inch thick cardboard, it is best to go to a specialized bookbinder or craft store who have the particular paper cutter needed for cutting cardboard. In printing works it is often possible to find someone kind enough among the cutters, if time permits, to cut your cover boards accurately for you. But if the thickness is $^1/_8$ inch, then they cannot help you, as they would damage the blade of their industrial paper cutter.

The best thing is to be independent, so get a utility knife and a rubber mat to cut through the various thicknesses.

mill board

grey board $^3/_{32}$ inch

cardboard for backing $^1/_{32}$ inch

PAPER

Paper is a material made from various vegetable fiber substances. Technically it is defined as the product from the process of joining the fibers together to make a uniform sheet of paper. The process can either be by machine or hand.

MACHINE MADE PAPER

Different types of paper are made by mixing together various glues and adhesives in different proportions. The following factors determine the vast range of paper types:

WEIGHT is measured in grams per square meter (1 meter = $1^1/_8$ yards) and is expressed by the figure g/m^2.

THICKNESS is derived from the low density of paper and from its, greater or lesser, compression capacity.

ASPECT is the aspect of the paper when looked at against light to see if there are any spots—uniformity means the quality is good.

RATTLE is the sound the paper makes when rubbed between the thumb and forefinger. Thanks to the experience gained when one becomes an expert, it is possible with this method to determine whether a particular kind of paper is suitable for writing or not.

It is always a good idea to examine the page's surface to make sure it is compact, even, and smooth.

SPECIAL CHARACTERISTICS

LAID PAPER has longitudinal and transverse lines that are visible.

WOVE PAPER has neither laid lines nor watermarks.

GLOSSY PAPER is shiny paper.

EMBOSSED PAPER has patterns in relief, textured cloth, leather, etc.

Laid paper is the type used in this book for the various projects.

PAPER FOR INSIDE PAGES

FABRIANO "VERGATONA" PAPER

This paper is from the Fabriano paper company.
It is used for the inside paper of day planners,
announcement cards, and invitations. The visible laid
lines, which recall ancient handmade paper, and its
particular surface grain are the main characteristics of
this machine made paper. It is durable and is available
in an ivory color. The sheet format is $27^1/_2$ x $39^1/_2$ inches.

FABRIANO "GRIFO" LAID PAPER

Also from the Fabriano paper company, this is a paper
of pure cellulose, wove, and laid. It is mainly used for
day planners and writing paper. It is available in various
weights and shades—ranging from white to ivory. The
formats are $27^1/_2$ x $39^1/_2$ inches or 25 x $34^1/_2$ inches.

FABRIANO "ROMA" PAPER

Produced entirely of cotton, this handmade, laid, and
watermarked paper has ragged edges all around and is
particularly suitable for quality publications and day
planners. Its ph is neutral, which prevents it from aging.
The sheets bear the C. M. Fabriano's logo on the lower
left, and, on the lower right, the word "Roma" is in an
oval. Its colors are named after artists such as Raphael
(sand colored) and Michael Angelo (ivory colored). The
format is 19 x 26 inches.

ART PAPER

Art paper includes all those papers suitable for painting
and drawing in general.
"Fabriano 5" is a quality paper obtained from 50%
cotton and 50% of other carefully chosen raw materials.
It is particularly good drawing paper for artists, architects,
and students because it especially works well with
watercolors, paint, charcoal, graphite, pastels, and wax.
It is white, and can be fine-grained, rough-grained, or
smooth-grained. Its weight ranges from 130 to 350
grams.

PAPER FOR FLYLEAVES

"Ingres," g 90/160 is the paper generally used for flyleaves. The surface grain and the fact that its color does not change with light are the main characteristics of this laid paper. It is suitable for quality publications, advertising graphics, and for those working in the paper industry and bookbinding.

The watermark reproduces the Ingres Fabriano logo and runs parallel to the two longer edges of the sheet. There is a vast range of colors: white, ivory, cream, sand, lobster, olive green, plum, blue ivory, ash red, grey, golden yellow, and black. The format is $27^1/_2$ x $39^1/_2$ inches.

INDUSTRIAL PAPER FOR COVERS

For covering books the market offers beautiful papers produced industrially that are available in speciality binding supply stores, well-stocked stationery shops, and fine art shops.

The variety of printed patterns is endless and ranges from papers reproducing classical designs (such as the Florentine or the Varese) to imitation leather types in cover tex, which are more suitable for covering booklets or register-type notebooks.

There are types of papers for all tastes. You will soon learn to choose which ones will work the best for your various projects. The following is a brief list of the papers mainly used in bookbinding:

"Varese": format $19^3/_4$ x $27^1/_2$ inches

Florentine style Varese paper: format $19^3/_4$ x $27^1/_2$ inches

Flowered type Varese paper: format $19^3/_4$ x $27^1/_2$ inches

French paper, marbled type: format $19^3/_4$ x $27^1/_2$ inches

French paper, normal type: format $19^3/_4$ x $27^1/_2$ inches

Fantasy paper: format $27^1/_2$ x $39^1/_2$ inches

HANDMADE PAPER

Over the last few years, handmade paper has become increasingly more popular. Craftsmen in both small workshops and in big paper factories manufacture it. Many artists view books as art objects within themselves and produce personalized paper using a variety of materials. Those photographed in these pages are by Lea Bilanci, a Florentine artist who makes vegetable paper by using raw materials such as herbs, flowers, and spices. Besides these, there are other types of paper made by combining various materials and glues until an original, eye-catching end product is achieved, such as waxed and tissue papers.

PAINTED PAPER

A further addition (still of an artistic nature) to paper consists in directly painting the paper sheets. In the photo on the right are some examples created by Maria Rita Macchiavelli.
Today it is possible to find an abundant variety in this sector and, if you wish to make yourself or others a journal, day planner, or personalized notebook, there is no end to your possibilities.

laurel paper

laurel paper

olive paper
(from the leaves)

wheat paper

nettle paper

painted papers

wheat paper

olive paper
(from the sprigs)

CLOTH AND PAPERS

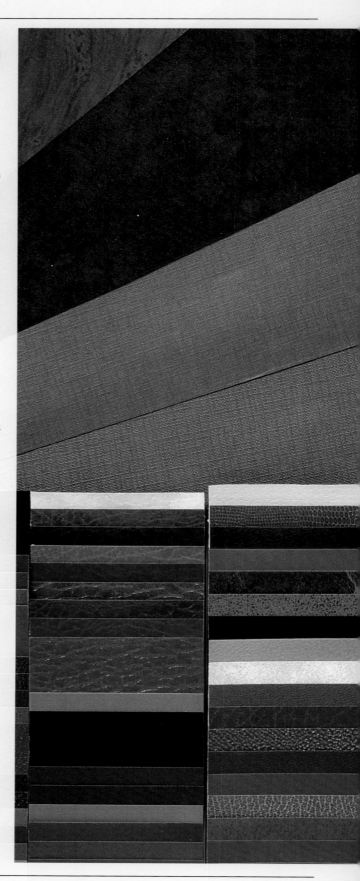

CLOTH FOR COVERS

For book covers, cloth, which is treated on the outside to make it waterproof and to prevent the glue from oozing out, is used. It is lined on the inside of the cover with a support of low-weight paper that is especially sized to make it stiff and make it less susceptible to dampness. Cloth for covers is available in various colors. The grain of the cloth may vary from fine, smooth, and rough. The following are some cloths that are widely used and which are the most suitable for covering covers:

EXTRA CANVAS

BUCKRAM

RAW FLAX

SETALUX

These cloths come in 39-inch wide roles and are sold by the yard.
While working, always take into consideration the grain and the axis along which the cloth is most flexible. It has to be kept parallel to the spine of the book.

PAPERS

The samples shown here present a wide range of embossed papers (leather texture) suitable for making notebooks, registers, and day planners.

SEWING WITH A SEWING FRAME

THE SEWING FRAME

Sewing frames are generally a wooden rectangular board that comes in a variety of sizes— between 16 to 20 inches long and 12 inches wide. The frame includes: two supporting screw rods, about 14 inches high, that are set into the base board at each side of the slit; a head beam that is inserted into the supports, which may be round or flat; and two split nuts that support the head beam and which, if rotated, permit it to be raised or lowered to keep the twines and tapes taut. Sewing frames usually have a bar that holds the binding thread in the lower part. If not, simply put in nails (or drawing pins) underneath the frame to block the twine or tape. Sewing frames can be found in bookbinding supply stores.

Try out your first binding project with a stool or a chair (see pages 132–139).

THE BOOK PRESS

This press is made up of two small wooden planks joined together by two supporting rods. A wooden or steel screw goes through the center of the two planks. The press is used to keep the volume under pressure while the spine is being sawed, or during other phases of preparing the book block.

OTHER MATERIALS FOR SEWING WITH A SEWING FRAME

The following are specific cloths for preparing the book block:

MULL is a fabric with loosely meshed threads that is used on the spine of the book. There are two types of mull: with paper or without paper. This fabric is mostly used in making book blocks.

CALICO is very sturdy and finely woven. Ordinary zippers are made of it.

PERCALE is a fabric with long fibers that are finely and closely woven.

CORDONNET is a yarn made of various silk or rayon threads that are tightly twisted together. It is used to create handmade headbands.

HEMP TWINE is attached to the sewing frame to sew the book. It is made of hemp strands that are twisted together (without adhesives). It absolutely must be of good quality so that it does not tear when being unravelled.

THREAD is sold in spools. Twist yarn, either with two or more twisted strands, is used for book sewing. It is made with cotton or linen. The numbers indicate the thickness—from number 10 (the thinnest) to number 60 (the thickest).

RIBBON is made of either silk or cotton and is used for bookmarks.

TAPE is available in various widths, the most commonly used are: $1/4$, $3/8$, $1/2$, and $5/8$ inches. There are, however, wider tapes of $3/4$, 1, and $1^1/4$ inches that are mostly used for sewing register type books. Colored tapes are available, but it is better to use natural ones because they last longer and are sturdier. A cotton band of twill is thinner and finer, and is used whenever the spine has no depth. Herringbone weave is stronger and is good for heavy and thick books.

HEADBAND can be found in different types (ready-made for example) and colors. Whether in silk or pure cotton, the headband is used to finish off the two ends of the book's spine.

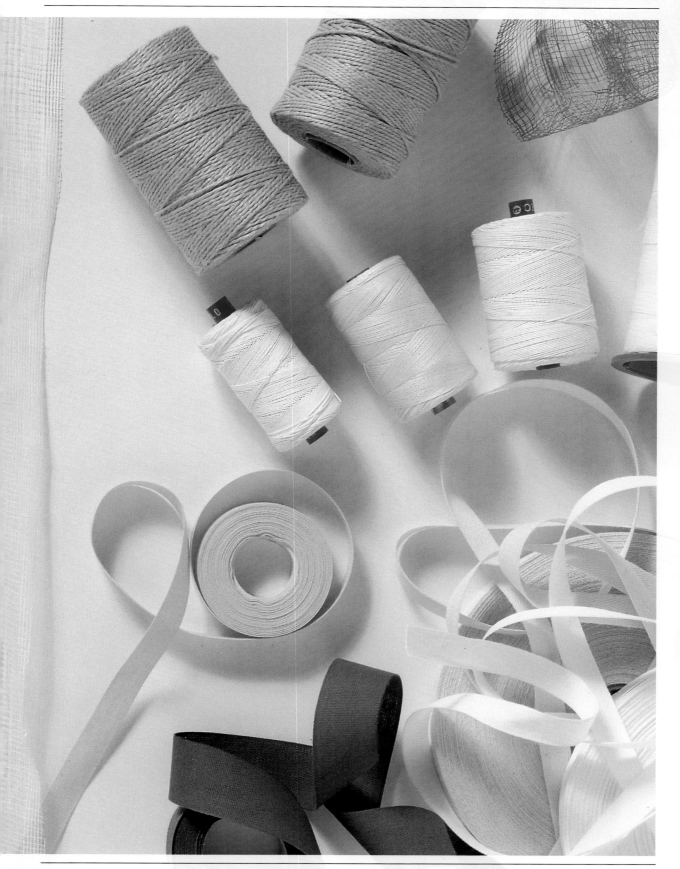

wooden rod for rounding the
back lining of the cover

VARIOUS TOOLS
AND ACCESSORIES

awl

unravelling board

scrubbing brush

brick or board for
pressing books

bookbinder's needles

bookbinding glue

beeswax

round and flat
paste brushes

vegetable glue

rubber mat

drawing pins

rounding hammer

staple remover

scissors

rubber
mallet

saw

BUSHMAN®
Art. no. E 150 - 250 mm
MADE IN GERMANY

file

bone folder

30

25

Utility knife

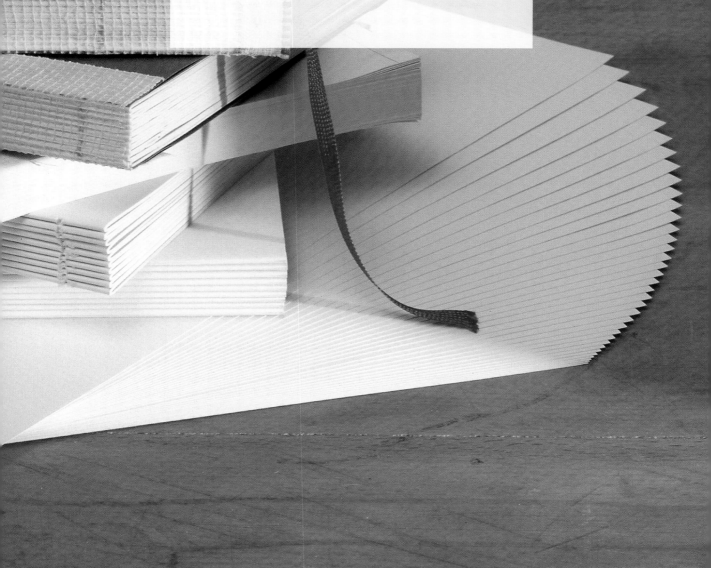

BASIC RULES

THE GRAIN OF THE CARDBOARD

The grain, or direction, of the cardboard is important for both the cover boards and for the backing.
Cardboard has an axis from manufacturing that enables it to fold and bend easily—this must be kept in mind when preparing the cover board because it must run in the same direction as the height of the volume. The way to determine how the grain runs is to "feel" it by doing some trial folding. The part that is the easiest to fold is very evident in the cardboard for the spine (even with $1/8$ inch cardboard there is no difficulty in finding it).

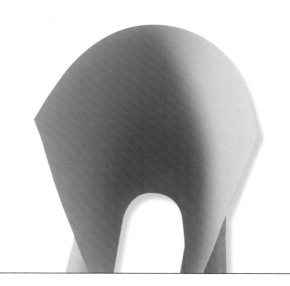

THE GRAIN OF THE PAPER

The paper's grain must be kept in consideration when gluing, cutting, and folding. To do bookbinding one must be able to recognize the axis from manufacturing. This must always run parallel to the height of the book so that you can take advantage of it when folding and gluing.
There are various ways of determining the direction of a paper's grain. Wetting the paper is the safest.

1

Take a piece of pre-cut paper and, using a clean paste brush, dampen the two perpendicular edges about a $1/2$ inch along their length. Wait a few seconds.

2

One edge will curl. The other will bubble at the border between the damp and dry areas because of the expanding fibers. This edge is the axis; therefore, the paper must be used with the vertical side in the other direction. The right part should be the one that curls.

ALIGNING THE PAPER

The loose or already sewn signatures need to be aligned often. This operation is essential and should be carried out while standing in front of your workspace.

1 *For a trial run take a ream of paper. Sort it out on your workspace.*

2 *Gather the sheets together and grasp them with your hands.*

3 *Bend the whole ream, pressing with your thumbs on the surface facing you.*

4 *If you pull the part held within your thumbs and leave the outer part loose, air will enter inside.*

5 *Tap the whole ream on your workspace and the sheets will align themselves.*

6 *With your now free thumbs, press the last sheets on the top, which are still outside the ream, back into line.*

7 *Tap the ream on your workspace once more.*

8 *Tap for the last time and, with all the sheets now in line, hold the ream steady and lay it on the table. The air that has entered could cause swelling. Hold the ream with one hand and with the other, pass various times over the surface of the block to press the remaining air out. The sheets are now aligned and squared.*

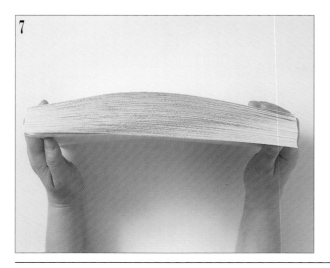

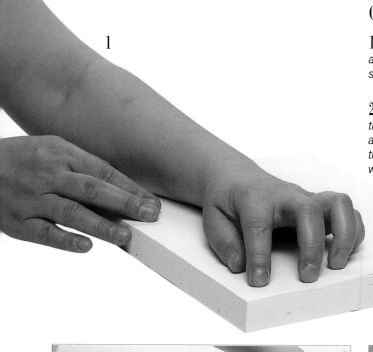

COUNTING THE SHEETS

1 *Align the ream and arrange it with the head-spine squared.*

2 *With the forefinger and thumb of your left hand, take about 20 sheets and lift them. Keep the ream steady with your right hand.*

3 *Rub the sheets facing you lightly but firmly between the thumb and forefinger of your left hand. Air will form between the first and last sheets.*

4 *Place your right hand on the raised part of the ream and position it from the cut part. Rotate your left hand along until you get as far as the center of the ream without difficulty.*

5 *Use the thumb of your right hand to count the sheets. Lower the sheets while the other fingers hold the paper steady.*

COUNTING FANNED SHEETS

This is a useful system when folding sections. Spread the sheets out like a fan. The sheets are clearly visible and do not have to be counted each time.

1

When the ream has been aligned, grasp the lower left-hand corner between your thumb and forefinger. Place the thumb of your other hand over the top right-hand corner so that the other fingers act as a support under the ream. Gradually release the grip of your left hand and let it slip towards your right.

2

When the ream is out of balance at the front, lightly close your right fist so that the outer part of your thumb leans on the sheets. Begin to skim over them without pressing too hard. This is not very easy but with one or two tries you will be able to make a nice fan.

3

Once the sheets are spread out in a fan, it will be extremely easy to take out five at a time, and folding will be a relaxing operation.

FOLDING THE SHEETS

1 *Take a sheet and hold it at the sides with both hands. Keep it straight and steady with your left hand while your right brings the sheet's edge towards the left margin. Make sure the sheet leans over delicately. Align the two sides well and also grasp with your left hand the part just folded.*

2 *Take the bone folder and place it at the center of the fold.*

3 *Crease the fold by passing the folder over it a couple of times.*

4 *The fold must be sharp and precise.*

GLUE

The adhesives used in bookbinding can be made of either natural or synthetic substances. According to the raw material involved, natural substances are divided into vegetable adhesives (starch paste and wheat flour paste) and animal adhesives, such as strong glue.

NATURAL ADHESIVES

Vegetable pastes specifically created for bookbinding are available on the market. They are not instant drying, are softer and more pasty than vinyl glues, and, once dry, can still be separated (which makes then essential when restoring or fixing damaged books). Also, they do not create a hard thickness and amalgamate well with paper and cords.

SYNTHETIC ADHESIVES

Polyvinyl acetate (PVA) white glue is the most used adhesive in industrial bookbinding. In craft binding it is mostly used in bindings without sewing. It can be used during all working phases and substitutes, more or less, natural adhesives.

DIRECT GLUING

This is used to attach cloth and paper to the cover boards.

Place the cloth to be glued on a clean sheet of waste paper. Hold the cloth steady with your tips of your finger. Hold the paste brush at the middle of the handle with your thumb on the tip. Spread the paste out in rays from the center and then outward. Each brushstroke must go right over to the waste paper underneath. When approaching the edge, lightly press to make the cloth adhere well to the waste paper. If you get to the edge and raise the brush, more often than not, you will also raise the inside of the paper and risk soiling it.

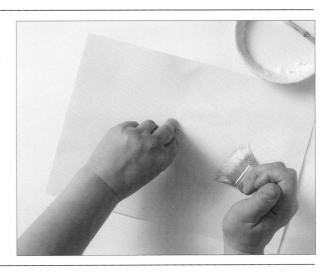

RIBBON GLUING

This means attaching various sheets that are glued only along a small fraction of their length.

1 Where only one sheet is involved, fold it and, having marked the surface to be glued ($^1/_8$-$^1/_4$ inches), place it between two sheets of paper or two pieces of cardboard. Only leave the part to be glued exposed. Keep everything steady with one hand and begin gluing with short brushstrokes towards the outside, passing from one end to the other.

2 If the sheets to be ribbon glued are more than one, lay the sheets over each other to create steps. Each step corresponds to the surface to be glued. At the top of the steps place a piece of cardboard, hold it steady with one hand and spread the glue with the other. The glue must not be either too liquid or too solid; otherwise, the work will not turn out exactly right.

SEWING

SAWING

Sawing is the operation that precedes sewing. It consists in making slots along the spine of the signatures. This serves both for sinking the cords within the spine and for making holes for the needle and thread to pass through. The cuts are made with a close-toothed saw and must be deep enough to get to the inside of the signatures. Make sure that the slots are neither too deep nor too shallow. Only experience will teach you the right depth and give you the right "eye". If the slot is too shallow, sewing will be difficult while if it is too deep, it will leave visible holes inside the signature. For the distances between the slots, keep to the measurements advised and always remember that the two end-point slots (for the link-stitches) are shallower than the inner slots (for the sunken cords). The end slots are also not to be widened with the file.

LINK-STITCH SEWING

This stitching is carried out on the two ends of the spine from the third signature on. It helps keep the signatures together by vertically joining them. It is very important and quite easy, though it may seem complicated.
The photo and drawing will make the operation clearer. It consists—from the third signature on—in passing the needle into the lower signature, inserting it crossways, and then pulling it upwards. In the stitching models here, we worked it so that the link-stitch, besides passing with a single thread, also knots around another thread. This is to keep the stitching more solid and sturdy.

 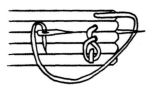

HALF-STITCH SEWING

This type of sewing consists in stitching two signatures at the same time but in an alternate manner. It is used for volumes of more than 20 signatures. The main aim of this type of sewing is to prevent extra thickness so that the spine will not arch too much. It can be used both on cord and on tape. Note that when using this type of sewing the first and last seven signatures are sewn in full-stitch so that when finished, the spine is narrower at the center but well sewn at the beginning and end of the book.
The drawings and photos shown here will help you to get the hang of the various steps. Have a trial run before actually binding a book. After the first seven signatures, take the two signatures and insert the bookmarks (one could be enough, but we have put in two to make things easier for you). The needle enters the lower signature through the hole of the link-stitch and exits from the following, always speaking of the same signature. With the next step, instead, we change to the upper signature, entering beyond the first cord or tape, which will show as being covered by a diagonal stretch of thread.
Return to the outside in correspondence with the second support. Go down again so that you enter once more beyond it in the lower signature. In this way we have alternated sewing, which passes along two stretches in one signature. This type of sewing reduces work time and speeds up your binding operations.

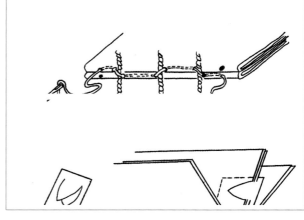

FULL-STITCH SEWING

This is called full-stitch because the thread passes through all the holes made, signature after signature (whether for sewing with three cords or with two). It is used for books of no more than 15–20 sections. The sewing sequence, which is fully explained in the 1st and 2nd projects, is as follows: The needle enters on the right through the first hole from the outside and then inward. It then exits diagonally at the side of the first cord and re-enters at the opposite side of the same cord until the last hole is reached. The length of the thread must be pulled at the end of stitching—the thread must always be taut. From the third signature on, link-stitching is carried out at the two sides until the last signature is reached, making double knots that are lodged inside the spine.

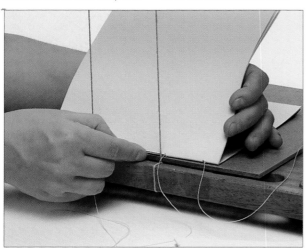

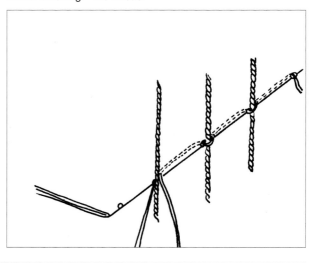

FLYLEAVES

This term is used to mean the two sheets that are the same size as the book block which are folded in half and placed at the beginning and end of a book. It protects the first and last pages of the book, those that are most likely to be damaged. Flyleaves also act as an intermediary between the book block and the cover and for aesthetic reasons concerning the gradual passage from cover to book proper.
Flyleaves must be of good quality paper and are somewhat thicker than the paper used inside the volume. The weight usually varies from 80 to 120 grams. Flyleaves may be prepared in various ways, but whatever the choice, the paper must always be arranged so that the spine fold coincides with its axis from manufacturing.

GLUED FLYLEAVES

This system is mostly used today in bookbinding because it is the easiest and quickest, though it is also the least sturdy. Glued flyleaves consist of a sheet folded in half and attached along the spine edge of the already sewn book by a light coat of glue that is spread along the fold. They may be the same size as the book pages or slightly bigger for trimming.

GERMAN-STYLE FOLDED FLYLEAVES

This type of flyleaf guarantees greater sturdiness in a book, though they are neither so easy nor so quick to make. They are good for simple but sturdy bindings.

1 *Cut a sheet to the exact height of the book and two and a half times the width of the signature.*

2 *Bring the right side of the sheet over on itself. Place a signature along the edge to act as a measure, mark a fold about $1/2$ inch from it and make the fold.*

3 *Turn the sheet and fold the left part, the shortest one, over the previous one. Fold very carefully. You will have a flap measuring about a half to a third of the volume.*

4 *Make the last fold on the other surface of the sheet, at a distance of $1/8$ - $1/4$ inch.*

5 *Fold with extreme care as the last fold involves three levels of paper. In order to fold the paper perfectly, you could pass over it with a ruler and a bone folder a couple of times.*

6 *You can check if you have made the fold properly by opening the sheet.*

7 *We have now obtained two flyleaves joined at the front and at the back by the folds.*

8 *Insert the first signature inside the narrowest fold (the last one made). The part with the flap is the one that will remain visible on the first*

signature and which will be attached to the cover boards.

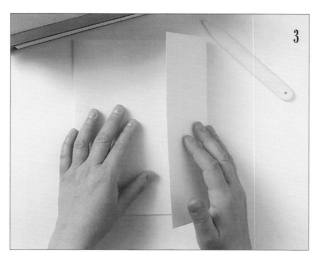

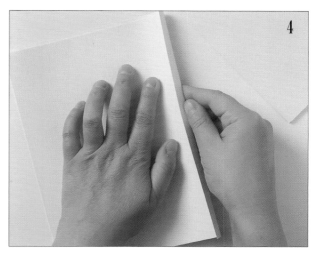

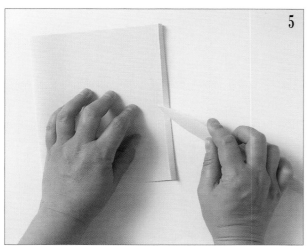

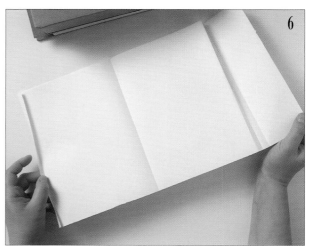

PROJECTS

HALF CLOTH AND PAPER JOURNAL

This journal, if its pages are left blank, is ideal for writing down your reflections every day.
You could also use it to keep track of your appointments and special meetings. If, instead, you add the dates,
you can turn it into a real day planner. In either case you will learn the basic rules of the bookbinder's art.
The characteristics of this first project are simple but at the same time very detailed
so that you can easily learn the technique step-by-step.

CHARACTERISTICS

- 150 pages (75 sheets, format 14 x $7^5/_{16}$ inches
- finished size $6^7/_8$ x $7^5/_{16}$ inches
- flat spine
- glued flyleaves
- full-stitching on two cords
- case cover with cloth corners

Difficulty: medium
Time: 4–6 hours

REQUIREMENTS

TOOLS
BOOK PRESS
SEWING FRAME
TWO BOOKBINDER'S NEEDLES
SAW FOR THE SPINE
FILE
BEESWAX
UNRAVELLING BOARD
FLAT BONE FOLDER
TWO WOODEN BOARDS ABOUT
10 X 14 INCHES
WEIGHTS (BRICKS OR WHATEVER
YOU HAVE HANDY)
BOOKBINDER'S GLUE
BOOKBINDER'S FLAT AND ROUND
PASTE BRUSHES
SCISSORS
SCRUBBING BRUSH (OR HARD BRUSH)
UTILITY KNIFE
RUBBER MAT
BLACK PENCIL
RULER
RUBBER MALLET

MATERIALS
16 SHEETS OF 100 GRAM IVORY
"GRIFO" LAID PAPER, FORMAT
27^1/$_2$ X 39^1/$_2$ INCHES
1 SHEET OF "VARESE," FORMAT
19^3/$_4$ X 27^1/$_2$ INCHES
20 INCHES OF BROWN CLOTH
20 INCHES OF MULL
TWISTED YARN N. 25
HEMP TWINE
HEADBAND
BOOKMARK

PREPARATIONS FOR SEWING

ALIGNING THE SHEETS

1 Ask your shopkeeper to cut you the number of sheets necessary for your journal in the desired format. Make sure they are accurately stacked and tapped so that it is easier to divide them into the five-sheet signatures that will make up the volume.

2 Grasp the ream with both hands and bend it. Keep your thumbs firm and bring the ream back to its original position. You will notice that when the sheets arch they all separate.

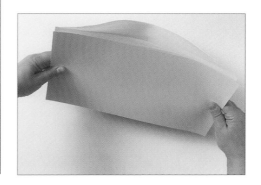

3 Keep this position and let as much air as possible enter between the sheets so that they arch and separate completely. To make it easier, sway your hands lightly.

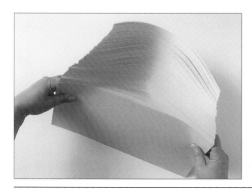

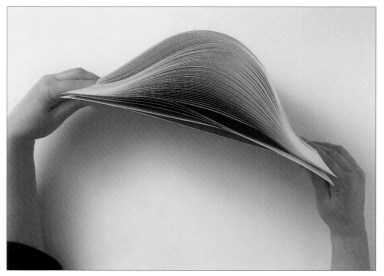

4 When all the sheets are separated, place the stack on the table and, before letting go, make sure that all the pages are in line.

5 Keep the stack steady with your left hand and, with your right hand, put a fair amount of pressure from left to right along the whole surface of the ream so that you eliminate all the air from the sheets.

6 Spread the sheets out in a fan. Hold the upper left-hand corner with your left hand. Let the sheets run through your thumb and forefinger. With your other hand, raise the ream at the lower right-hand corner. Let the sheets slip towards the right until they have fanned out a bit.

COUNTING AND FOLDING THE SECTIONS

7 With the flat bone folder or the thumb of your right hand, let the sheets slide until they have formed a fan.

8 The sheets are now far enough apart from each other and are ready to be picked up in the desired number. With your right hand, grasp five sheets and lift them carefully from the fan.

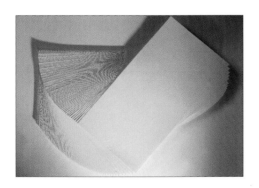

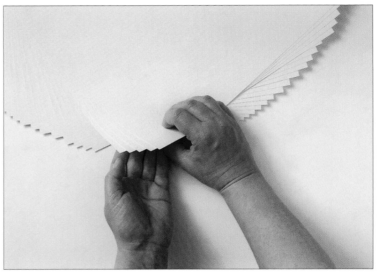

9 From now on use the bone folder to fold the signatures in groups of five sheets. Take the first signature and tap it once or twice on the table to align it.

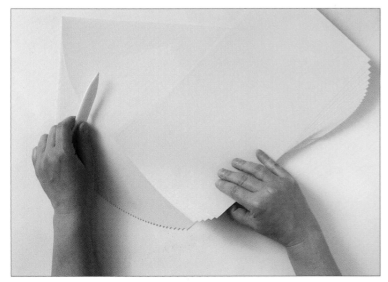

10 Hold the signature upright and fold it in half, aligning the edges of the sheets as much as possible. Then place the signature on the table, keeping the pages steady with your left hand.

11 Hold the signature steady and make a fold with the bone folder. Go over it various times until the fold is sharp and precise. Repeat this operation with all the other signatures. You should have 15 at the end, equal to the 150 sheets, which will make up the volume.

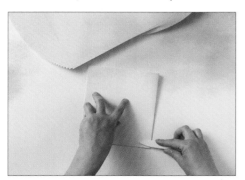

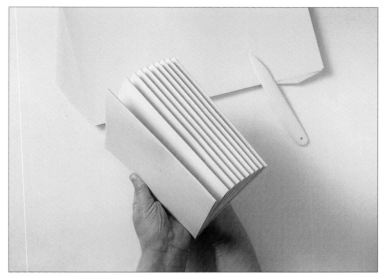

12 Pick up five signatures at a time and, using the rubber mallet, hammer them along the fold. Insert the whole book block between two wooden boards and press it with two bricks or another type of weight.

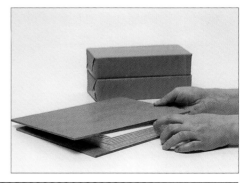

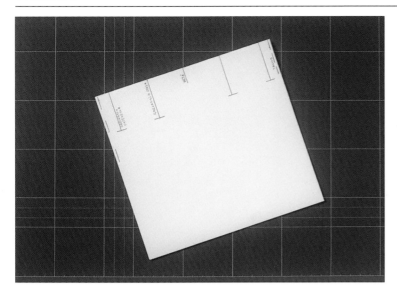

SAWING

1 On a sheet as big as the pages of the volume to be sewn, trace the measurements of the slots you will make with the saw. Proceed as follows: make a guide mark at the center of the sheet. From this trace, respectively to the right and to the left, another two guide marks at a distance of 1³/₄ inches. Starting from the left border of the sheet, make a guide mark at ¹/₄ inch and another at ³/₄ inch. Starting from the right border, make a guide mark at ¹/₄ inch and one at 1 inch. You have now created a template for making four slots, i.e. two end-stations (for the head link-stitch and the tail link-stitch) and two for the sunken cords.

2 Take two ¹/₈-inch thick sheets of cardboard and cut them a little bigger than the sheet format. On these supporting bases, which will protect the outer signatures during sawing, place the template. By following the guide marks previously traced out on it, you will create the slots for the sunken cords.

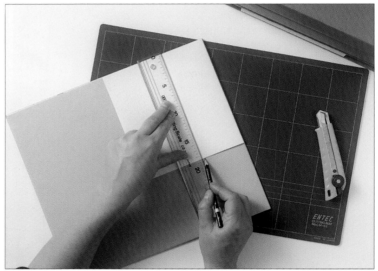

3 On the cardboard trace out the dimensions of the sheet with a ruler and pencil. With the utility knife, cut the cardboard along the non-graded side of the ruler. Perform this operation on the rubber mat.

4 Position the signatures between the two pieces of cardboard, tap them into alignment along the spine, and insert the book block into the press.

5 Tighten the press. When the block is firmly clasped, place the template with the measurements on the first piece of cardboard. With a pencil, reproduce the distances previously marked. Do the same with the other piece of cardboard.

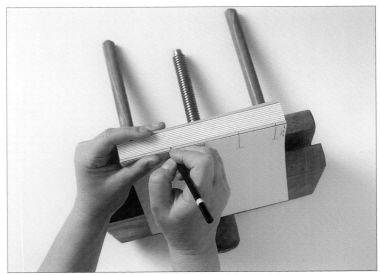

6 Hold the spine of the volume firmly in one hand. With the other, grasp the saw and begin cutting in correspondence with the guide marks traced on the two pieces of cardboard. When sawing the slots, which must be only a fraction of an inch deep, use the saw in one direction only, from the outside towards you. In this way you will avoid tearing the paper. Continue like this until the four slots are clearly visible.

7 When the sawing is finished, slightly widen the two central slots with the file, as they will hold the sunken cords. This will make it easier to sink the cords into the slots without creating a thickness or hump along the spine.

8 Before extracting the block from the press, slip the cord into the slot to make sure it fits properly. If it does not, widen the slots again slightly with the file. Take out the block, open the signatures, and check the holes. You can improve the holes with the help of an awl.

GLUED FLYLEAVES

9 To prepare the flyleaves choose a colored paper. The type of paper or color is not important (though it should match with the inside of the book), but it must be sturdy and heavier in weight than the paper used for the other sheets. Remember that the flyleaves are double (at the head and tail of the volume) and each consists of a sheet folded in half. Before cutting them, check the run of the paper's grain. Then, with a ruler and pencil reproduce on the flyleaves the measurements of the volume.

10 With the ruler and the utility knife, cut the sheets cleanly and precisely. Place the flyleaves with a ribbon of edge showing, with the part to be glued measuring 1/4 inch. Coat with a little bit of glue.

11 Glue the first flyleaf onto the first sheet of the volume, keeping it a distance of about 1/8 inch from the signature fold. Even if the journal's pages are not numbered and this operation seems quite easy, do not be deceived. Caught up in the work you could easily mistake, for example, the grain of the flyleaves, so be sure to fold and position the sheets properly. The right side of the paper must remain inside.

12 Repeat this operation at the end of the volume, gluing the flyleaf on the last sheet of the last signature. Place the journal under weights and let dry.

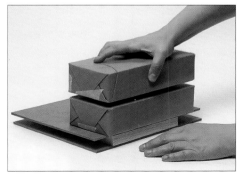

SEWING

PREPARING THE SEWING FRAME

1 Cut two pieces of hemp twine that are long enough to be tied into nooses to the frame's head beam. Cut another two pieces of hemp twine about 23⅝-inches long and knot them to the two nooses.

2 To position the first twine, place a sawed signature on the base of the frame.
Pass the first twine along the inside slot of the signature, then in the slit in the base of the frame.

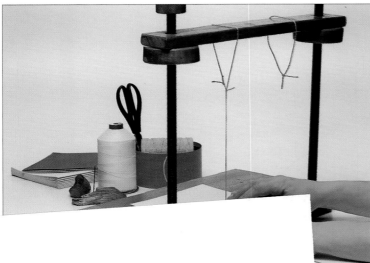

4 Wrap the second twine in the same way, remembering that both must correspond exactly to the slots in the signatures. When this is done, pull the twine taut by screwing the two split nuts at the top of the frame. Both twines must be taut.

A "length of thread" means the quantity of thread needed for sewing. This is the formula: with the thread, measure the height of a signature and multiply it by the overall number of the signatures. For our project you may expect to sew the whole volume with one length. Before threading the needle remember to wax the thread so that you will avoid making knots while sewing.

SEWING

5 To facilitate sewing the first signatures, insert a piece of wood between the base of the frame and the first signature (which will be the last with respect to the sequence of the book). Position the first signature to be sewn (the flyleaf remaining underneath) making the two central slots correspond with the cords. From this point on, in order to carry out the link-stitching correctly, follow the instructions given on page 42. Sew by inserting the needle into the first hole on the right, leaving at least 4 inches of thread hanging, which will later be the link-stitching. While you are sewing with your right hand, keep the signature steady with your left.

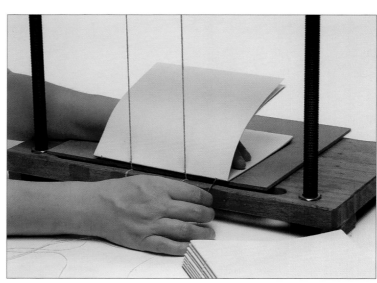

6 Take the needle out through the second hole, twist it around the twine, and insert it into the same hole. With your left hand remove the needle from the third hole. Grasp it with your right hand, pass it over the second twine, and insert it into the third hole. Remove it from the fourth hole.

7 Put down the needle and press the signature with your hands. Put in the second signature, position it correctly, and sew it, beginning this time from the fourth hole (i.e. where you left off from the previous sewing operation).

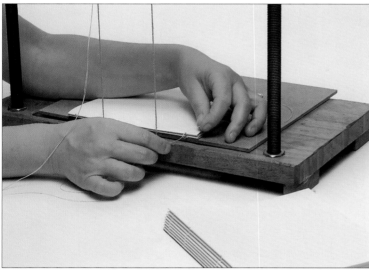

8 When you have completed the second signature, put the needle down. Align the signatures and pull the thread so that the sewing is taut. Press the signatures with your hands to make them slip along the twines. Knot the thread you are sewing with to the 4-inch piece of thread that you left hanging at the beginning.

9 Cut a piece of thread that is about 8 inches long and thread another needle with it. Insert it at the head, between the first and the second signatures, passing around the thread attached to the fourth hole. Leave a strand of about 4 inches hanging.

10 Make a double knot. This thread, which will hang for about 4 inches, like the one left at the beginning of sewing, will serve to make the double link-stitch. During these work phases refer to the instructions on page 42.

11 Arrange the third signature in place and repeat the sewing operation, starting from the right, where you had finished sewing the second signature. When the thread has come out of the fourth hole (the one at the head) take up the two strands from the previous sewing and raise the thread that was knotted between the first and second signatures.

12 Pass around the link-stitch thread with the needle, making it pass between the first and second signatures. Pull strongly to keep the three signatures together. Pull upwards until the knot is taut and well flattened. This is a very important step and is carried out at each end of each signature, as already mentioned.

13 Continue in this way until all the signatures have been inserted, being careful to refer during each work phase to the instructions given under BASIC RULES. Remember that while sewing, the needle (so as to direct it each time to the following hole) passes repeatedly from the outside inward, from one hand to the other, without the signatures being opened.

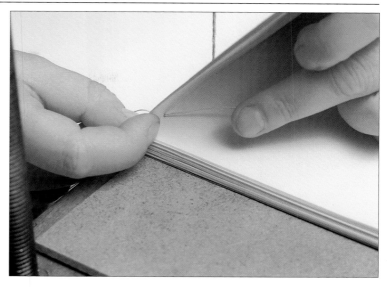

14 You will soon notice that the difficulty in sewing consists in the mechanical gesture of passing and re-passing the needle inside and out without looking. Thanks to this simple process, you will gain more confidence in the work you are doing. Your hands and the needle, working in harmony, will proceed quickly and mechanically.
A small tip for sewing without looking: listen to the "sound" that the needle tip makes when it meets the hole.

15 When you have reached the last signature, repeat the step of the link-stitch, passing the needle inside the signature that is underneath (see photo). Pull the thread and flatten the signatures. Unthread the needle and make a tight, flat double knot.

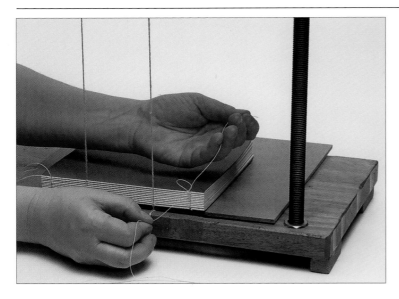

16 Make a knot at both sides of the book and cut the thread, keeping two strands about 2–2¹/₂-inches long.

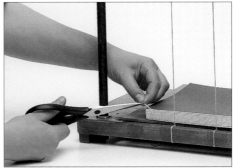

17 The book is now sewn. When the sewing is finished, the signatures should be perfectly aligned, and the book should look compact.

18 Remove the volume from the frame by cutting the twines from underneath. Leave them about 2¹/₂-inches long. Then cut those tied to the head beam and leave them the same length.

MAKING THE BOOK BLOCK

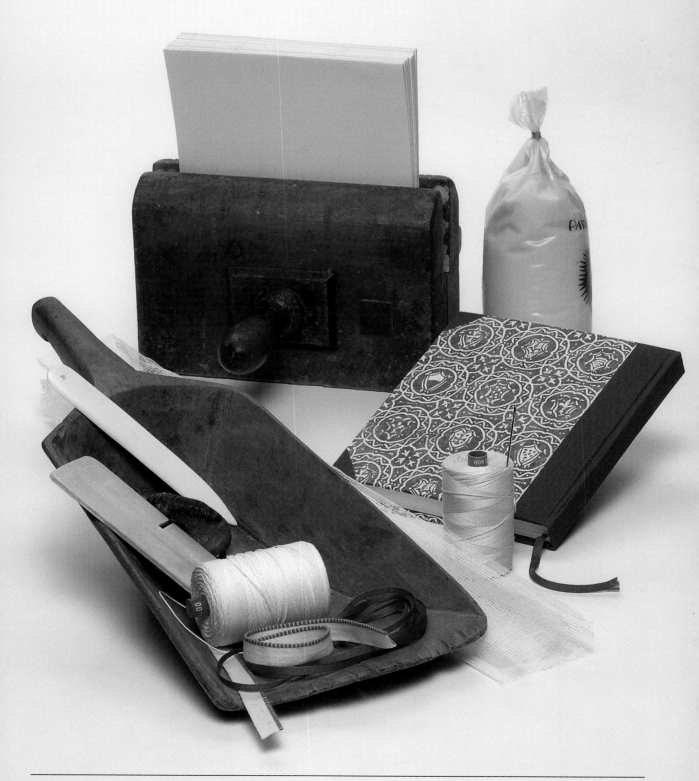

TIGHTENING THE TWINES

1 This operation consists in pulling the sewing twines taut, using the spine as a lever. In this way the volume will turn out better "bound" and more compact.

2 When they have been pulled, shorten the four pieces of twine to about ³/₄ inch. Untwist the strands (about two or three).

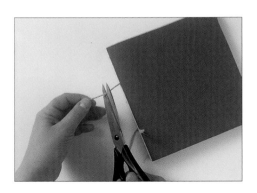

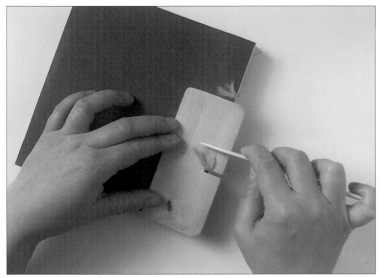

3 Take the unravelling block, insert a strand of twine at a time and, using the bone folder or a blunt knife, unravel the four pieces of twine until they look like small tuffs of cotton wool. Then shorten them by ¹/₄ inch.

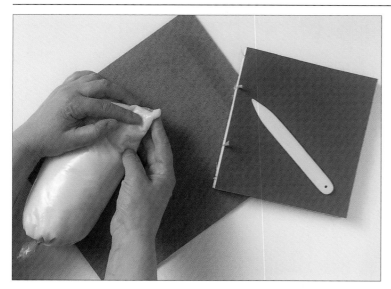

4 Paste the four tuffs with bookbinder's glue until they are well saturated. Then lay them on the flyleaves with the help of the bone folder and flatten them.

5 Still using the bone folder, work the fragments until they are quite flat. This way you will avoid unsightly bumps at the end of the work.

GLUING

6 When the twine has been glued, place the volume on a wooden block (or on waste paper) to prevent soiling your workspace. Position the book at the edge of the table and glue the spine. To level the coat of glue properly and to avoid it from ending up on the visible part of the flyleaf, use an even–edged piece of cardboard.

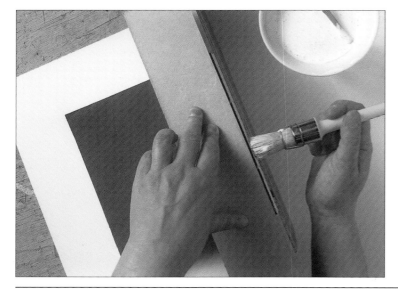

7 Place it under pressure and let dry. In the meantime cut a strip of mull (the type with paper) the same length as the height of the volume and 1¹/₂-inches wider than the spine.

8 Shield your workspace and spread the glue onto the paper side of the mull. Let it dry for a few seconds. Do not overdo it with the glue, as unsightly dribbles could occur.

9 Remove the weights from the volume and, without moving it, begin gluing the mull, making sure it protrudes ³/₄ inch at the sides of the spine.

10 Using the scrubbing brush, brush lightly along the mull surface so that, softened by the glue, it will penetrate as much as possible into all the crevices and adhere perfectly to the spine.

11 Place the volume under pressure once more and let it dry. Cut off any excess mull and get ready to finish off the book block and to attach the bookmark.

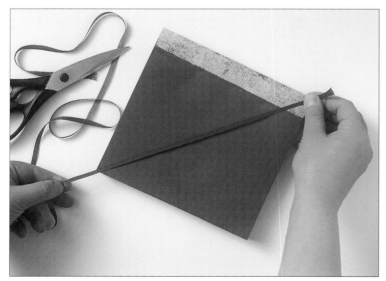

12 To measure how long to cut the bookmark, hold the string diagonally over the book surface and add about 4 inches. Cut, spread a little bit of glue over one end of the bookmark, and place it at the head of the book at the center of the spine. Press hard for a couple of seconds.

13 Now start applying the headband. You can choose whatever weave and color you prefer. The headband acts as a "frame" at each end of the spine. To measure it properly, lay it across the spine of the book.

14 Spread a layer of glue on the headband and let it dry for a couple of seconds. Then place it at the head of the spine. To do this properly, hold the book against your chest at the side opposite the spine. Press to make it stick and cut it with a scissors.

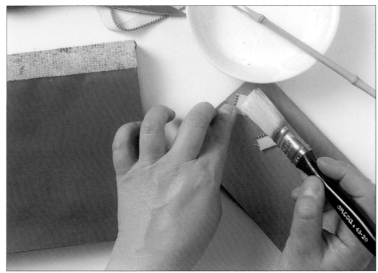

15 Repeat this operation at the other end of the spine. The book block has now been completed—sewn, finished off, and ready for its cover.

THE CASE COVER WITH CLOTH CORNERS

MEASURING THE COVER

1 With a ruler, measure the width of the volume from the spine to the edge of the pages. Subtract $1/16$ inch from this. Then measure the height and add $1/4$ inch.

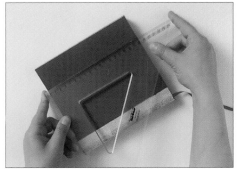

2 To cover the spine, measure its width and subtract no more than $1/16$ inch. Measure the height of the volume and add $1/4$ inch.

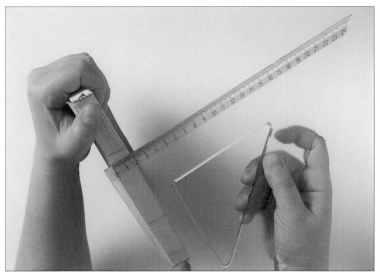

CUTTING THE CARDBOARD

3 Place the cardboard on the rubber mat and make sure it is perfectly aligned. Make on it all the previously taken measurements—those for the two cover boards and those for the spine.

4 Carefully cut, making sure that the utility knife is always in a perpendicular position. Hold the ruler absolutely steady as you work as even a fraction of an inch out of line will affect the appearance of the journal.

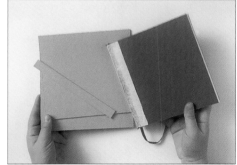

CUTTING THE CLOTH

5 Cut the cloth which, in this project, will be used to cover the spine and the outer corners of the cover. When cutting the cloth, first check the run of the grain. For the measurements, add $2^1/_2$ inches to the width and $1^1/_2$ inches to the height. The extra dimensions will be used for the turn-ins on the top, the bottom, and the side.

6 Also cut 4 small rectangles that are $1^1/_4 \times 4$ inches to cover the corners of the volume.

CUTTING THE PAPER

7 Begin cutting the "Varese" paper for the cover. Trace on the back of the sheet the measurements of the cover boards and of the spine. Add 1½ inches to the height. This extra part will be used for the turn-ins. For the width, subtract ½ inch from the measurement since ¼ inches of the cover are taken over by the spine cloth.

8 Note that since the cloth used for the spine overlaps the cover boards for 1¼ inches, the paper of the cover will overlap the cloth for at least ¼ inch, thus leaving 1 inch visible. Take the cloth, fold it lightly in half, and make a small "V"-shaped snip at both ends.

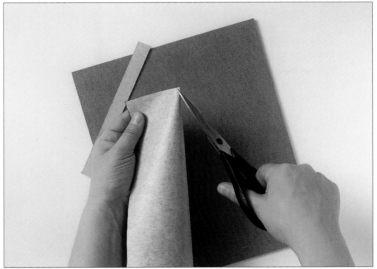

9 On the back of the cloth at the center of the rectangle marked by the "V"-cut, trace the two vertical lines that make up the outline of the book's spine. At ¼ inch distance from each line, draw another two. These will be used for placing the cover boards and creating the groove, the furrow between the spine and the cover that allows the book to open properly. This phase of the work should be carried out on a perfectly flat block of wood.

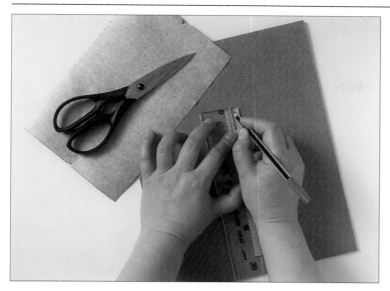

10 For correct positioning, also mark the center of the cardboard spine. Make sure that the marks are clearly visible.

GLUING THE CLOTH

11 With a flat brush, spread the glue all over the surface of the cloth where you have traced the guide marks. Let it dry for a few seconds and then take the cloth and transfer it to a clean surface.

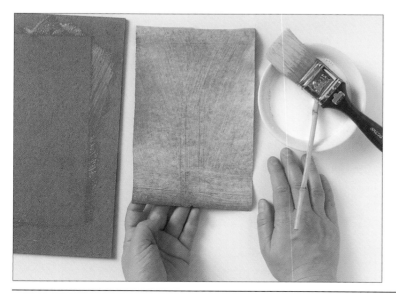

12 It is important to let the glue dry for a few seconds before attaching the various parts together. Since bookbinder's cloth becomes dirty easily, be sure your workspace is always clean.

13 You will see that when the glue has dried properly it leaves the previously made guide marks clearly visible. Take the cardboard spine and make it stick along the outline traced on the cloth.

14 Now that the guide marks are clear again, start attaching the cover boards as well. Do this with firm movements and the cloth will follow your hand easily. Remember that lines traced at $1/4$ inch from the spine are the exact gluing positions.

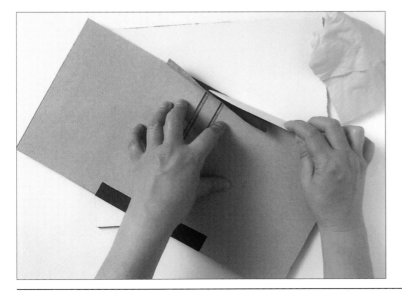

15 Quickly turn in the cloth—at the head and the tail of the book—using a bone folder and a clean cloth. Pull the two strips of cloth well and flatten them various times with the bone folder, using an outside-to-inside movement.

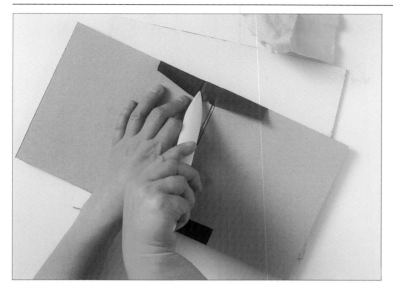

16 With the edge of the bone folder, pass over the cloth that corresponds with the grooves (to make them visible). Attach all the cloth to the cardboard and clean the bone folder each time after use.

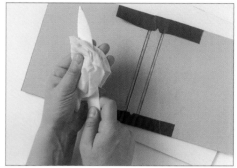

17 Turn, and then turn again the cover, head, and tail so that you can work on the two cloth head caps at the same time before the glue has completely dried.

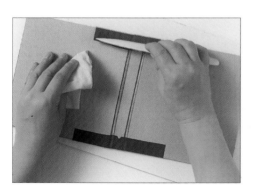

18 Before starting to glue the printed "Varese" paper, lift the cover and check that it is properly aligned and that the ends match perfectly.

GLUING THE PAPER

19 Before gluing the paper onto the cover, you must make on the glued cloth a guide mark of $1/2$ inch (maximum of $3/4$ inch) from the outer margin on both surfaces. It is at this point that the paper is glued and overlapped onto the cloth. To do this you could use the bone folder, but a good bookbinder will know how to impress the point directly with his or her thumbnail.

20 Take the printed "Varese" paper that was previously cut out. Place it face down on the wooden block and spread it with glue, beginning from the center. With a "bicycle spoke" pattern, glue right up to the edges. Take the paper from the wooden block, transfer it to a clean surface, and let it to dry for a few seconds.

21 When the paper has completely dried, place it onto the cover and attach it. Position it height-wise so that it protrudes $3/4$ inch at the head and the tail.

22 When the inner side of the paper has been attached, do not let it lie on the whole cover surface, but attach it by passing backwards and forwards with a clean cloth. Doing this eliminates all of the air bubbles.

23 If there are still any air bubbles left when the work is finished, do not worry. Burst them with a needle and rub over them with the bone folder and a clean cloth.

24 Turn the cover over to the inside. With sharp scissors, cut the paper at the corners, keeping about $1/8$ inch away from the corner tips. This measurement should be, more or less, the same as the thickness of the cardboard used for the cover.

25 When the paper has been cut along the corners, turn in the upper strip with the bone folder. Make sure that each corner tip has been well covered. The extra paper remaining must be pressed down.

26 Turn in the lower strip also. When both corners have been turned in, fold the side strip as well and attach it, using the bone folder.

27 Check that the three turn-ins are properly glued. If not, add a few more drops of glue. Repeat these turning-in operations also for the second part of the cover. Let dry. In the meantime, spread a coat of glue on the four small rectangles, which are to cover the corners of the journal.

28 When the glue is dry, hold the cover and glue the first two rectangles to the corners. Attach them so that a small fraction protrudes beyond the tip of the corners.

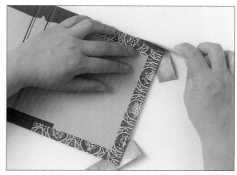

29 When turning in the cloth at the corners where it is exposed, you must attach the protruding pieces very precisely by flattening them and by making them adhere along the thickness of the cardboard. When the corners have been glued, see if the book block can be cased into the cover.

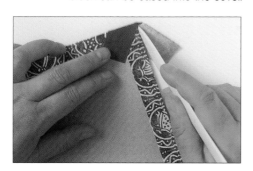

POSITIONING THE BOOK BLOCK

30 Open the cover and lay the sewn book block onto the cover board to your right. Check that the cover protrudes by the same amount at the three edges of the volume. This protruding strip is called the "projecting edge."

CASING

31 Before attaching the book block to the cover, have a trial run at casing. With your right hand, hold the book block steady on the right cover board. With your thumb and forefinger of your left hand, lean on the spine to press it over the book. Raise the left cover board and let it drop. The board should fall.

32 To keep your work clean and neat, place a sheet of waste paper between the flyleaves. Take the glue and spread it over the surface of the flyleaf to be glued inside the cover.

33 When you have finished gluing, take the waste paper away and let the glue dry until it becomes transparent. Without moving the book from the position it is in, keep it steady from the right side and lift the cover, pushing it a little (for the position of your left hand see photo 31).

34 Close the book from the left. If all the measurements and various operations have been carried out properly, the cover will fall with a slight puff, which is a sign that tells you the closing is perfect.

35 Keep the book closed for a few seconds. Open it and, if there are a few creases, use the clean cloth or the bone folder to smooth them out. Turn the book, and repeat the gluing operation on the other side as well.

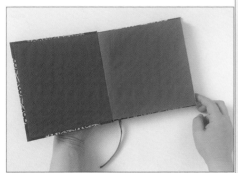

36 Check that this part is also properly completed. Place a sheet of waste paper between the flyleaves, close, and let the volume dry completely. After about an hour, your journal is ready for your own use or as a gift.

HALF CLOTH AND PAPER JOURNAL WITH A ROUNDED SPINE

This second project will give you a chance to practice the sewing technique you already tried.
You will learn the art of rounding (rounded spine) and how to make German-style double flyleaves.
This journal is made with a different format and pattern than the first project. The working phases, already tackled in the previous project, will now be less detailed. The new steps, on the contrary, are given greater attention.

CHARACTERISTICS

– 100 pages (50 sheets, format 13 x 9 inches)
– finished size $6^{1}/_{2}$ x 9 inches
– rounded spine
– German-style double flyleaves

– full-stitch sewing on two cords
– case cover

Difficulty: medium
Time: 5-6 hours

REQUIREMENTS

TOOLS
SEWING FRAME
BEESWAX
NEEDLE
SAW
UNRAVELLING BOARD
FLAT BONE FOLDER
SCISSORS
RUBBER MALLET
ROUND WOODEN ROD
FILE
BRICKS OR WEIGHTS
SCRUBBING BRUSH
BOOKBINDER'S FLAT AND ROUND
PASTE BRUSHES
BOOK PRESS

MATERIALS
14 SHEETS, FORMAT
27$^1/_2$ x 39$^1/_2$ INCHES
IVORY "VERGATONA", 130 GRAMS
$^1/_8$-INCH THICK CARDBOARD FOR
THE COVER
$^1/_{16}$-INCH THICK CARDBOARD FOR
THE SPINE
20 INCHES OF RED CLOTH
1 SHEET OF FRENCH PAPER,
13$^1/_2$ x 20 INCHES
20 INCHES OF MULL (WITH NO
APPLIED PAPER)
BOOKBINDER'S GLUE
TWISTED YARN NUMBER 0
HEMP TWINE

PREPARING FOR SEWING

ALIGNING THE SHEETS

1 Take the stack of pre-cut sheets, bend it in a "U"-shape and, holding the first sheet steady, bring it back to its original position. The arching allows the sheets to be separated.

COUNTING THE SECTIONS

2 Spread the aligned sheets out in a fan, and begin counting the sections (i.e. the signatures consisting of five sheets). Fold them with the bone folder, following the instructions in the previous project.

3 When all the necessary sheets have been folded, tap them with the mallet along the fold and flatten them as much as possible. Put the folded signatures under a weight.

DOUBLE FLYLEAVES

4 Cut two sheets of the same type of paper the same height as the signatures, but two and a half times the width of the folded signature, i.e. 16 inches. To make German-style flyleaves, follow the instructions on page 42.

5 Bend the sheet without defining the fold, bringing the right part $5/8$ inch beyond the measure of the signature, i.e. 7 inches. When it is in line, fold it with the bone folder.

6 Rotate the sheet so that the extra part is on your right-hand side, and fold it from the outside inward. Pass the bone folder over the fold to make a sharp crease.

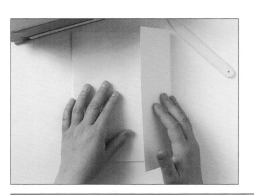

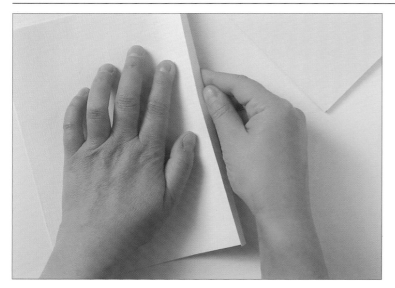

7 Turn over the sheet from bottom to top. With the bone folder, mark the distance of ¼ inch from the right edge, and fold. This third fold must be very well creased.

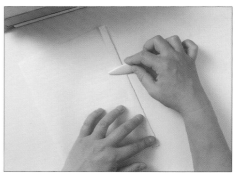

8 You can see if the fold is well creased by opening the sheet. Repeat the same operation on the other sheet.

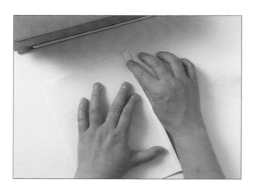

9 Insert the first signature inside the narrowest fold (the last made). The part with the flap is the one that will remain visible on the first signature and later adhere to the cover boards.

10 Spread a coat of glue inside the third fold of the flyleaf to make it stick to the signature. This will allow the first signature (and the last) to be easily sewn to its relative flyleaf.

SAWING

11 Insert the signatures between two pieces of cardboard and put them into the book press. Mark on a sheet, and then on cardboard, the measurements of the slots (head, center, and tail), keeping in mind the size of the book's format and the number of sunken cords used (in this case it is again two).

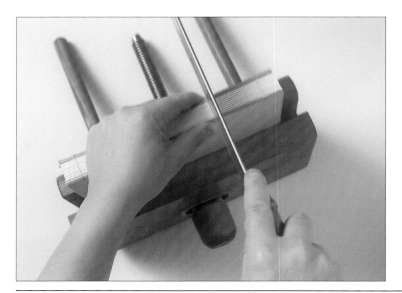

12 With the saw, cut the four slots (two for the head and tail link-stitches, and two for the cords). The slots should be $1/8$-inch deep.

13 With the edge of the file, slightly widen the two central slots (those for the sunken cords) like you did in the previous project. Take the signatures from the hand press and check that all of the pages are pierced. If they are not, use an awl to make the holes. Place the signatures in the book press once more, being careful to align them properly.

SEWING

14 Arrange two pieces of hemp twine into nooses on the head beam of the frame. From these, extend two pieces of twine and attach them to the frame's base. Line up the first signature and, by twisting the two split nuts, make the twines taut. Begin with the last signature (the one at the back of the book). Wax the thread and then thread the needle. Insert it into the first hole on the right, remembering to leave out a strand of thread about 4-inches long for the right-hand link-stitch.

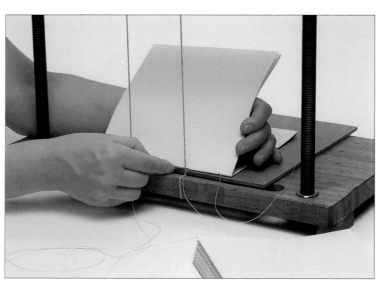

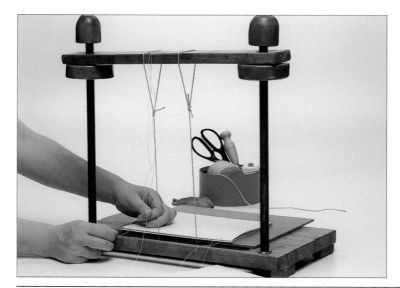

15 When you have come to the end of the second signature, draw the thread tightly and make a knot on the right side. Insert on the left the thread for the link-stitch. When you have put in the third signature, make the left link-stitch, lifting up the thread that keeps the first two signatures together.

16 Before making the link-stitch, remember to pull the yarn well to the side. The needle must always pass under the previous signature and cross the thread, which is kept raised.

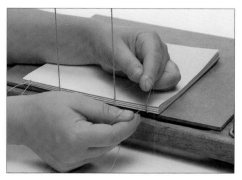

17 Proceed in this way to the last signature. Press the volume with your hands. Though these operations are monotonous, they are essential for successful sewing.

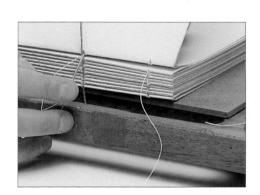

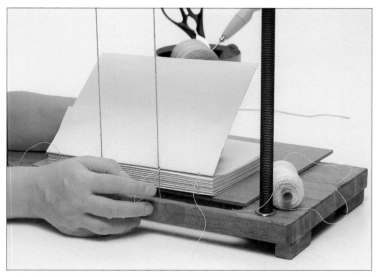

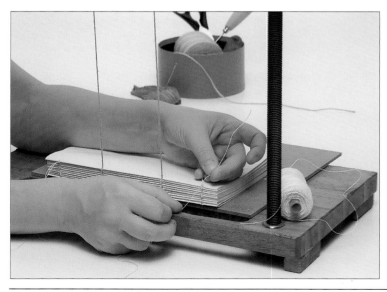

18 When you have sewn the last signature, tie a double knot and cut the thread, leaving a little bit extra. Take the book from the frame and cut the twines so that you have two 2$\frac{1}{2}$-inches long strands.

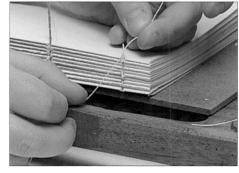

MAKING THE BOOK BLOCK

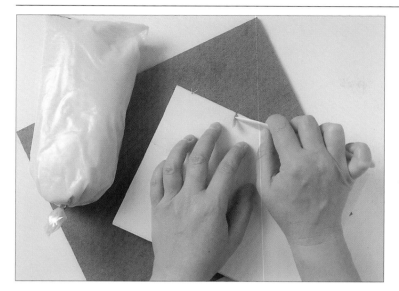

TIGHTENING THE TWINES

1 Divide the strands that make up the twine and, with the help of the unravelling board, make them into a tuff. Cut them $\frac{1}{2}$-inch long, saturate them with glue, and spread them with the bone folder so that they are completely flat against the flyleaves.

GLUING

2 As you did in the previous project, place the volume on a sheet of waste paper and, shielding the upper part with cardboard, spread the glue along the spine with the round paste brush.

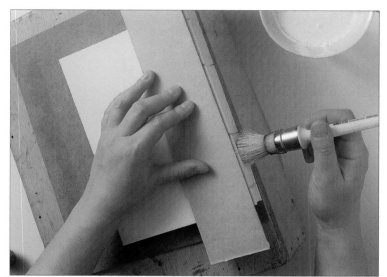

3 Put the block under a weight and wait about 15 minutes. When rounding, the spine must not be completely dry. Separate the flyleaves on the front with a paper knife.

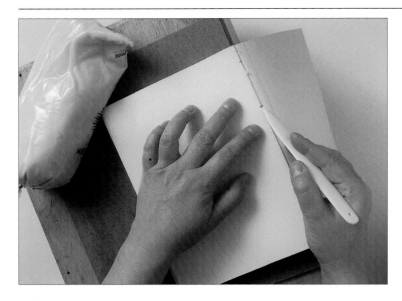

ROUNDING

4 Before beginning the rounding, open the book at the end (tenth page) of the first signature where you glued the flyleaf. Check that the stitching has held. Should there be any small openings, spread a light coat of glue with the bone folder. Let dry. Repeat this operation on the last page of the last signature.

5 Place the volume along the edge of your workspace and grasp it by the first 10–15 pages. With the side of the mallet, softly strike from the center of the spine to the head, so as to round it. Turn the volume over and repeat the operation on the other side.

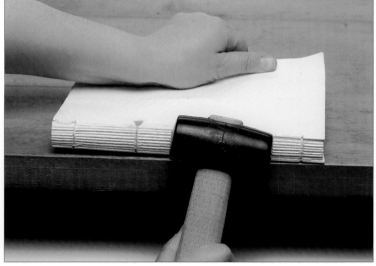

6 Just a few blows will suffice for the spine to take on the shape you give it. The important thing is not to overdo it—the rounding must be evident, but not too much. With this in mind, check the block from the edge of the pages. The recess of the fore-edge must look nice.

7 Prepare the strip of mull by cutting it the same height as the volume and 1¹/₂-inches wider than the spine. Spread glue on it. Let dry for a few seconds and then attach it to the book. With the scrubbing brush, make the mull penetrate into all the folds of the spine. When the mull has been attached, tap the spine again a few times.

8 For the German-style flyleaves it is best to snip the flap to avoid, as much as possible, any extra thickness. Therefore, make some cuts where the twines are situated, stopping a fraction of an inch from the spine.

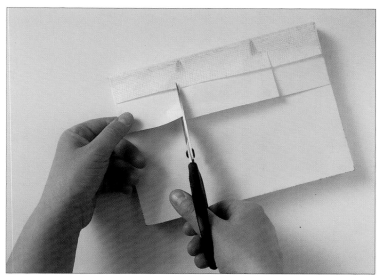

9 Continue by cutting the corners at each end of the flap. Do the same with the flap at the end of the volume. Cut the bookmark and the headband. Glue them on and let dry.

CASE COVER

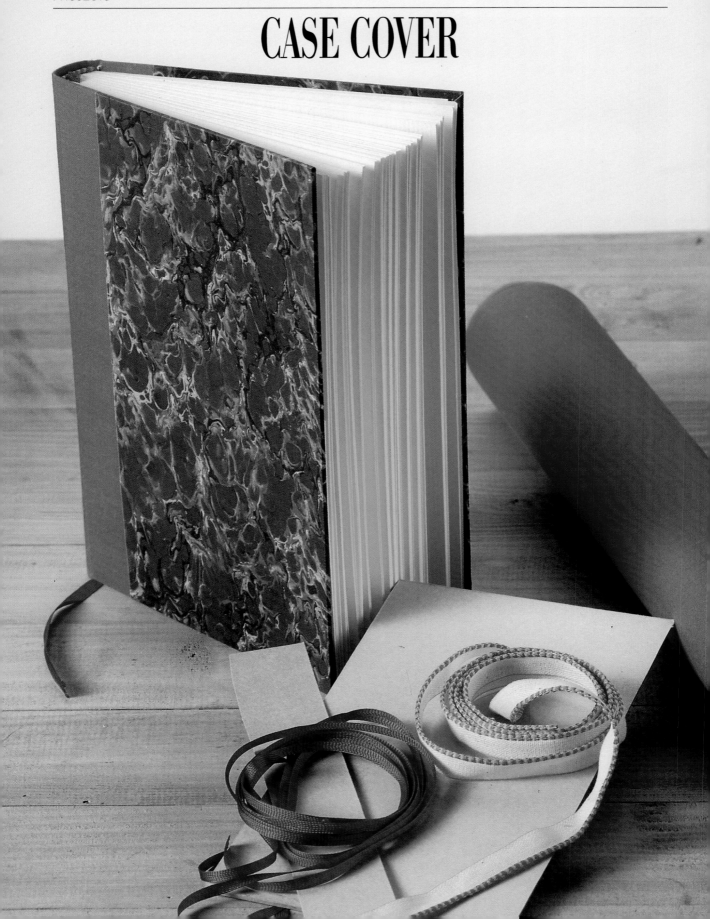

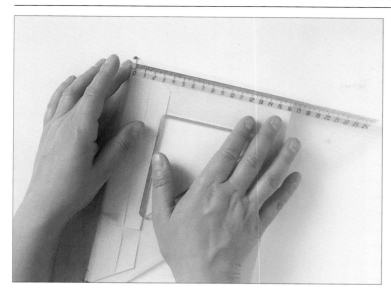

1 Measure the book block. Reduce the width by 1/16 inch and increase the height by 1/4 inch with respect to the book's format.

2 When measuring a round spine it is a good idea to use a piece of twine or paper so that the measurements will be exact. Take a piece of twine and, holding the book against your chest, measure the swell of the spine.

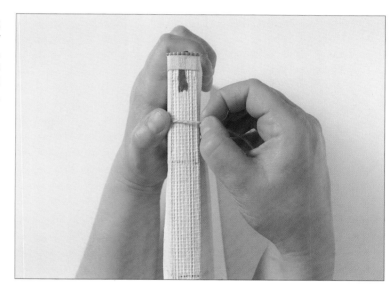

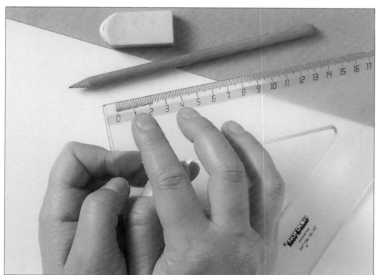

3 Mark this measurement on a ruler and prepare the cardboard for the cover (1/8-inch thick) and for the spine (1/16-inch thick). Cut the cloth for the spine and the paper for the cover, remembering to leave an extra 3/4 inch for the turn-ins.

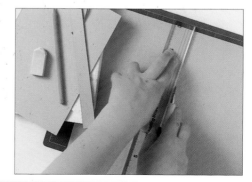

4 Check the grain of the cloth and cut it after having marked on it the measurements of the center and those of the grooves (at a distance of $1/4$ inch). Spread the glue on the cloth, let it dry a little, and attach the spine. At $1/4$ inch along the side lines for the grooves, place the two cover boards. Do the turning in at once, before the glue dries.

ROUNDING THE SPINE

5 Lay the spine of the cover on the round rod. With the palm of your hand, apply pressure backwards and forwards to round it. To make sure that the result is successful, check that the grooves are clearly evident and that the ends of the cover match perfectly.

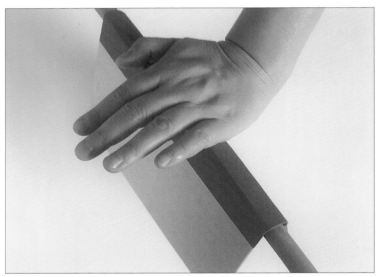

6 At $1/4$ inch from the left and right borders of the spine cloth, mark with the bone folder the points where you will glue the cover paper. Spread the glue on the back of the paper, let it dry very briefly, then position it on both the cover boards. Attach it using a clean cloth.

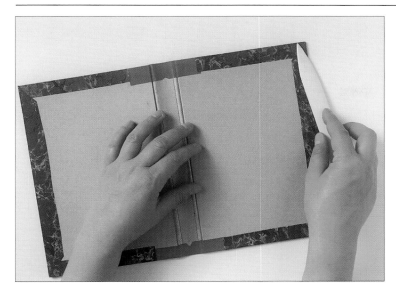

7 Turn in all the sides very quickly, pressing the corners well (this journal has no cloth corners so the paper must adhere perfectly). Case the book block into the cover and check that the projecting edges on the three sides are uniform.

8 To ensure the casing is successful, it is a good idea—at least for beginners—to first glue the flap of the flyleaf and see that it adheres properly to the inside of the cover. Then you can glue the actual flyleaf itself.

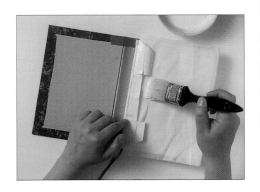

9 Turn the book around, keeping it compact and closed, and repeat the operation for the end flyleaf. After a few seconds check that the flyleaves are taut. Let it dry for an hour.

BINDING PUBLICATIONS INTO A BOOK

The project in these pages is made up of 80 instalment issues. By binding a book made up of so many elements you will learn the sewing technique called "half-stitching". As two issues are bound at the same time, the stitching is carried out half on one and half on the other. The result is a spine that is not too swollen and quite uniform. Thanks to this technique you will be able to bind by yourself, and with great satisfaction, the numerous publications that come in instalments. Usually the covers and flyleaves are sold readymade with the issues, but if you would like a special cover, this project offers instructions for choosing one according to your own taste.

CHARACTERISTICS

– half-stitching or alternated
  sewing on three cords
– cloth cover

Difficulty: medium–hard
Time: 6–7 hours

REQUIREMENTS

TOOLS
SEWING FRAME
STAPLE REMOVER
SAW
RUBBER MALLET
SCRUBBING BRUSH
FILE
FLAT BONE FOLDER
UTILITY KNIFE
SCISSORS
A FLAT AND A ROUND PASTE
BRUSH
BEESWAX

MATERIALS
20 INCHES OF MULL (WITH OR
WITHOUT PAPER)
BOOKBINDER'S GLUE
HEMP TWINE
1 YARD OF COLORED
BOOKBINDER'S CLOTH
CARDBOARD FOR COVERS
HEADBAND

SEWING

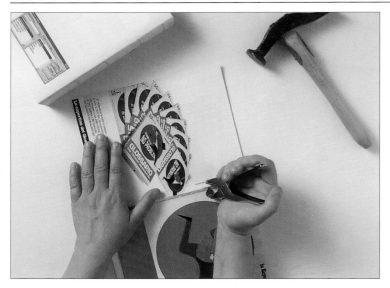

1 When binding printed publication issues that are to be sewn together, pay special attention to the numbering of the pages and the sequence of the chapters. The first thing to do, therefore, before beginning work is to put all your issues in the proper order. With the staple remover extract all the staples holding the pages of each issue together. Even if you intend on using your own cover, do not throw away the covers of the various publications.

2 When all the staples have been taken out, set out the issues in their proper order. You will see at once that they are inclined to arch along the spine, so you will need to use pressure and some hammering with the mallet. Place them on a sturdy workspace and hammer them in groups of five.

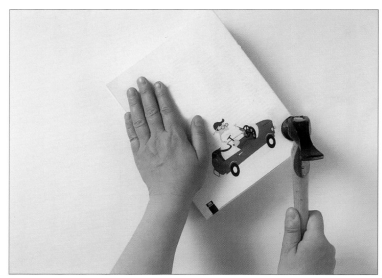

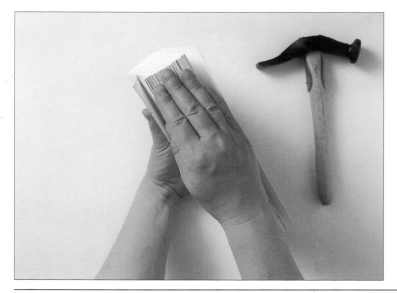

3 Place the issues once more in their proper order. Cut two sheets of cardboard $1/8$-inch thick and a little wider than the page format. Insert the whole block of issues between these two cardboard sheets.

4 Align the whole block and slide it into the book press (keep the spine on the bottom). Tighten well and keep the block under pressure for one night.

5 Take the block from the book press and put it back in again, this time with the spine facing you. Begin the usual procedure for sawing.

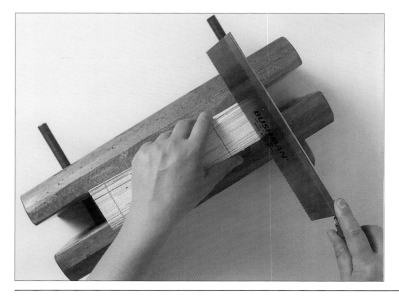

6 Use the flyleaves, which usually come with the publications, or make them yourself by following the instructions previously given. Mark the slots for sawing. Remember that stitching on three cords is involved; so, you must make two slots for the link-stitch stations (at the ends of the volume) and three for the sunken cords (one in the center and two at about a 2 inches distance).

7 Before beginning the sewing, make two bookmarks from cardboard. In the center of these, cut a small tongue and raise it. When inserted into the center of the issues, the bookmarks will make the alternated sewing easier. To make them follow the instructions given on page 45.

8 Position the twines on the sewing frame in correspondence with the slots. Pull them taut. Wax the sewing thread and thread the needle. Be careful to arrange the issues in their proper order and avoid (it has happened!) putting them in upside down. Start, therefore, from the last issue and be sure all of the first pages are always facing you.

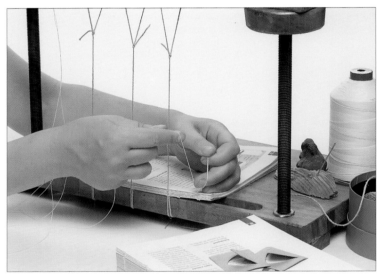

9 The first seven issues are sewn full-stitch to make the volume more sturdy and compact. Proceed with the work that you did for the journals. When you arrive to the eighth issue and before you thread the first hole, insert one of the card bookmarks into the center of the signature and start sewing. Run the needle through the first hole and out through the second—you will find that you are at the right side of the first twine.

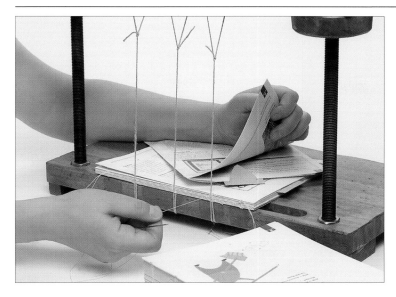

10 Take the following issue, insert the second bookmark in the center, and start sewing. Inset the needle into the second hole at the left side of the first twine, encircling it.

11 Sew the issue until you exit at the next hole (to right side of the second twine). With your left hand, raise the center of the last issue that you inserted (photo below) and enter the needle into the hole at the left side of the second twine.

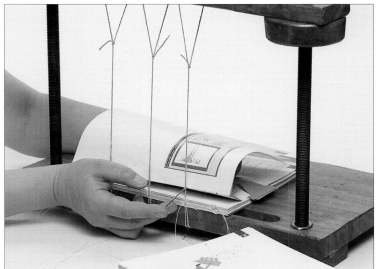

12 Bring the needle out at the right side of the third twine of the last issue you inserted. Remember to always pull the thread a little (even though at this phase the thread must run fairly loosely).

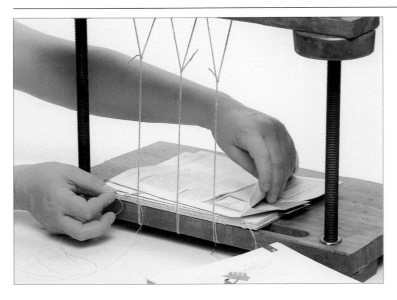

13 Insert the needle once more at the left side of the third twine and exit it through the last hole of the link-stitch (of the last issue inserted). Pull the thread and flatten the issues.

14 Continue sewing with the link-stitch, pulling the thread upwards. Make sure that the spine is aligned. Take the next issue.

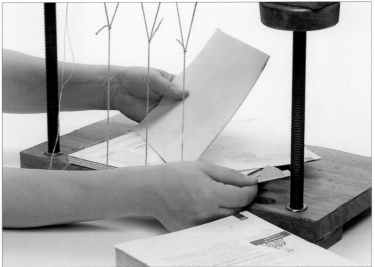

15 Repeat the previous operation. Place the card bookmark at the center of the issue. Sew starting from the left. Insert the next issue.

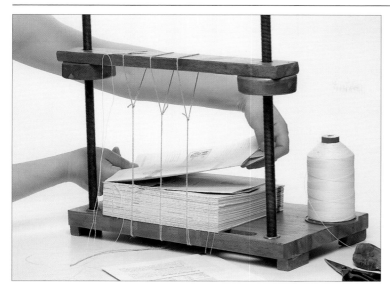

16 Continue in this way until you reach the last three issues. Always let the bookmarks help you.

17 Take out the bookmarks and sew the last three issues using full-stitch to make the volume sturdier and more compact. Remember to do the link-stitches at the ends and to pull the thread. When you reach the end, make a double knot. Take the book from the book press and cut all the twines, leaving them about 2 inches long.

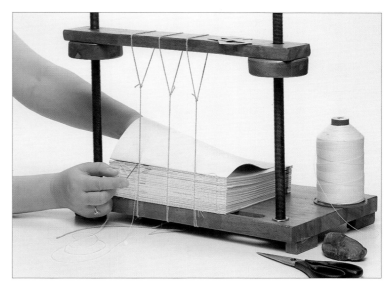

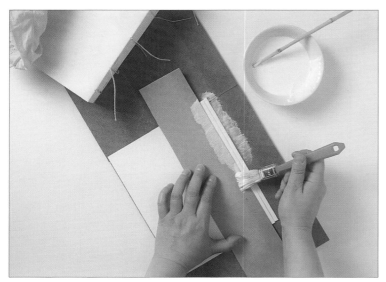

18 With glue and a flat paste brush, ribbon glue the flyleaves at the head and tail. Do this on a sheet of waste paper or on a wooden board. Attach the flyleaves, keeping them about 1/8 inch away from the spine.

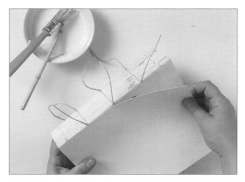

19 Untwist the strands that make up the twine and unravel them with the bone folder and the unravelling board. Saturate them with glue and flatten them at the sides of the flyleaves by pressing them with the bone folder.

20 With the round brush, spread the bookbinder's glue along the whole spine. Rub until the spine has soaked it all in. When this is done place the book under weights and let it dry.

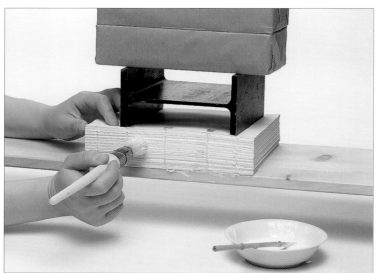

21 Spread glue onto the mull band, which is used to strengthen the sewn spine. Let it dry for a few seconds. Then, apply it along the whole spine, making it adhere well with the scrubbing brush. Cut the headband and glue it to the two ends of the spine. The book block is now ready to be cased into the cover.

THE CLOTH COVER

If a cover has come with the issues, carry out the casing of the block by following the steps shown in the previous projects.
If, instead, you would like to create your own cover, buy cardboard and 1 yard of colored cloth and follow the instructions in the next couple of pages.

1 Cut the cardboard for the cover boards and for the spine, remembering that you must add ¼ inch to the height and subtract ¹⁄₁₆ inch from the width. Begin cutting the cloth. Since it will need turn-ins, it must be cut 1½-inches longer and wider than the cover format.

With a ruler and pencil, trace on the cloth the measurements of the spine, side grooves, and both cardboard cover boards. Spread the glue in a "bicycle spoke" manner. Take off the cloth immediately and place it on your perfectly clean workspace. Let it dry for a couple of seconds.

2 When the glue has dried, place the central spine and then the two cover boards on the cloth. Beginning at the head, quickly turn in the extra cloth with the bone folder, making sure to flatten the corners well. Turn in the cloth at the tail of the cover and then the side strips.

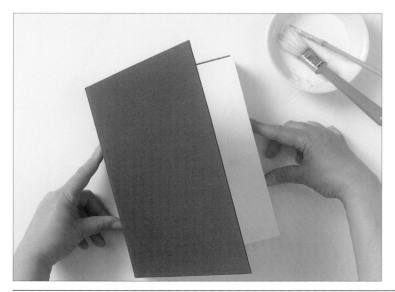

3 Case the book block into the cover, glue the flyleaves, and close the book while keeping it steady. Let dry. After an hour open the cover and flick happily through the pages of your book.

BINDING BY SEWING ON TAPE

This project consists in binding issues intended to form a collection (publications) using the technique of sewing on tape instead of on cords or twine. Since the number of issues is small (10 altogether) and they are heavy, full-stitch sewing is used. The flyleaves and cover become an integral part of the issues themselves.

CHARACTERISTICS
– sewing on three tapes

Difficulty: medium
Time: 4–5 hours

REQUIREMENTS

TOOLS

SEWING FRAME
SAW
SCRUBBING BRUSH
FLAT AND ROUND PASTE BRUSHES
STAPLE REMOVER
FLAT BONE FOLDER
PINS
SCISSORS
BEESWAX
NEEDLE
DRAWING PINS

MATERIALS

NATURAL HERRING-BONE TAPE
TWIST YARN, NUMBER 25
MULL (WITHOUT PAPER)
BOOKBINDER'S GLUE
HEMP TWINE
HEADBAND

SEWING WITH TAPE

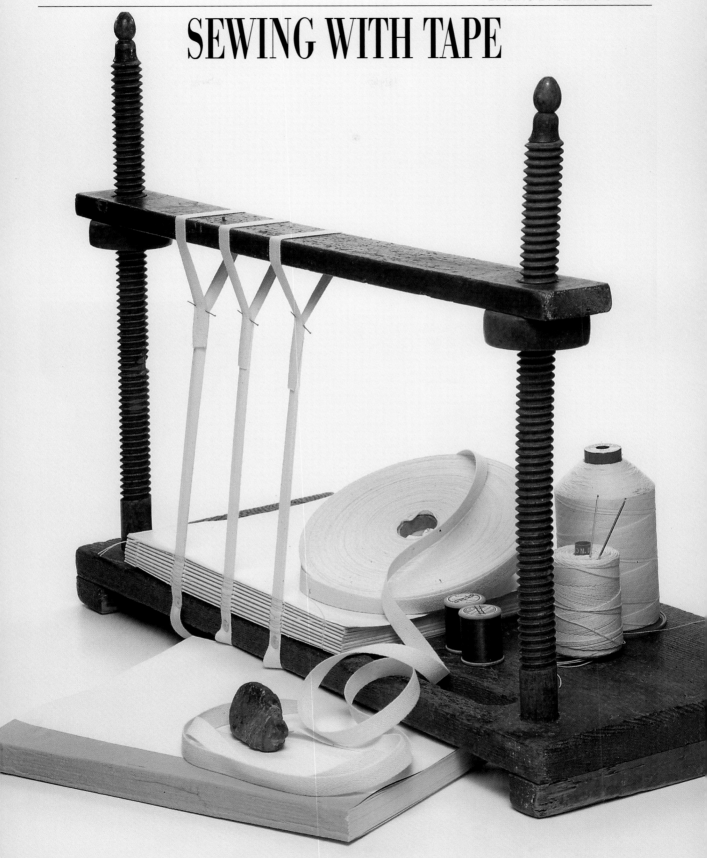

1 As printed issues are involved, it is essential to keep them in their proper numerical order. Take out the staples, overlap three issues at a time, and hammer along the spines to flatten them out.

2 Insert the book between the two protecting pieces of cardboard, previously cut. Place the book in the book press from the side of the spine, tighten, and keep it under pressure for at least 24 hours. Then tap and square.

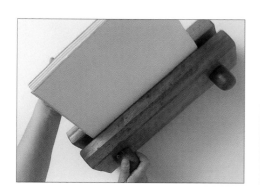

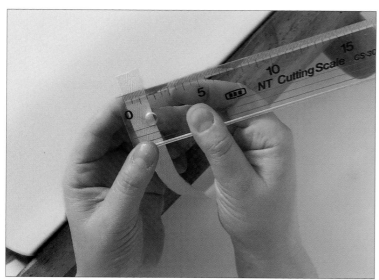

3 To obtain the width of the slots for sawing, measure the width of the tape, which is usually $1/2$ inch. Remember that the book will be sewn along three pieces of tape.

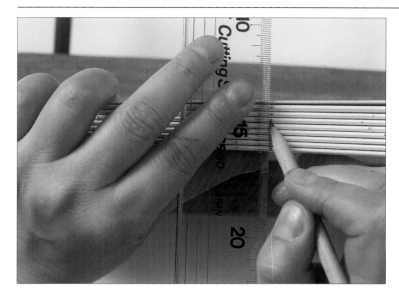

4 Calculate the measurements for sawing. Mark at the center of the spine the first guide mark for the slot that will hold the central tape. Make another two guide marks (one on the right and one on the left) 1³/₄ inches from the central point. The guide marks for the link-stitch stations have to be made at ³/₄ inch from the left edge for the head, and 1 inch from the right edge for the tail.

5 Saw the slots as in previous projects. The slots must be ¹/₈-inch deep. Since they do not have to hold the cords, it is not necessary to widen them with the file.

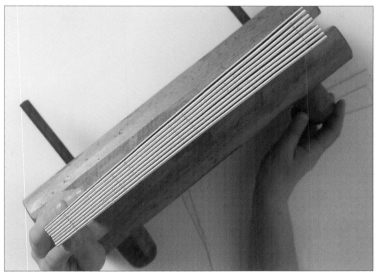

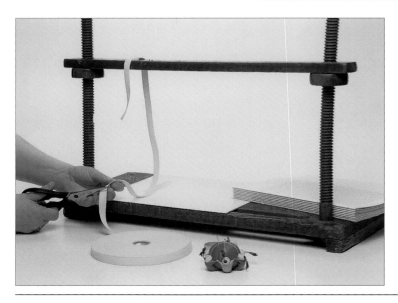

6 When sewing on tape, the tape must be keep absolutely taut on the sewing frame. There are frames with special devices for this, but you can make do with drawing pins and ordinary pins.
Begin cutting the three pieces of tape.

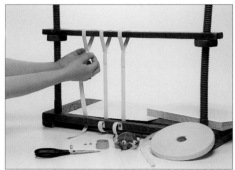

7 Attach the three tapes to the frame's head beam. Form a noose on each one, which you can block with pins. Position the first issue (the last within the book) and make the tapes coincide with the three central slots.

8 Attach the three pieces of tape to the base of the frame, using some drawing pins. When the tapes are perfectly in place, turn the split nuts and make the tapes taut.

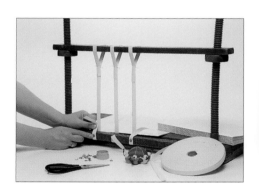

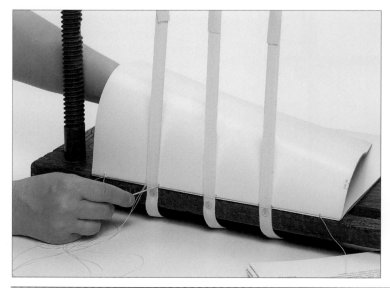

9 Before beginning to sew, measure the proper length of the thread, wax it, and thread the needle. Enter the first hole, leaving out a piece of thread about 4-inches long that you will use with the link-stitch.

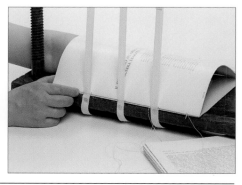

10 With the second issue, add the thread for the link-stitch at the left end. This will keep the issues joined together at both ends. Work carefully, remembering to pull the thread upwards. Make sure that the knot is inside the spine.

11 Continue in this way until all the issues have been sewn. Make the link-stitch and flatten the whole volume well. Finish off with a double knot.

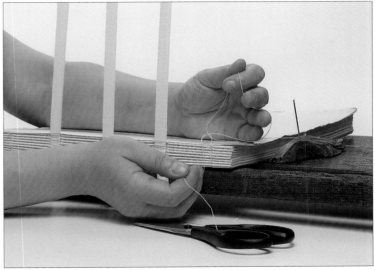

12 Cut the sewing thread and take the book from the frame. Remove the drawing pins. Cut the tapes but let three strips hang out at least 2-inches long.

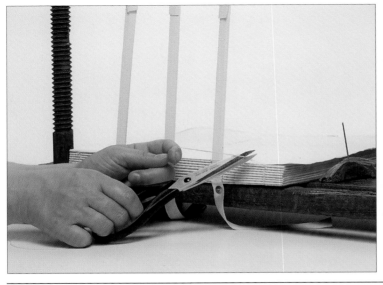

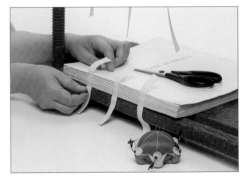

MAKING THE COVER

1 Spread a ¹/₄-inch wide strip of glue along the borders of the flyleaves. Make sure to protect the rest of the surface with some cardboard or waste paper.

2 When the glue has somewhat dried, raise the tapes and glue the flyleaves on the first and last pages of the volume, keeping about ¹/₈ inch away from the spine. Let it dry well. Then, glue on the tapes as well.

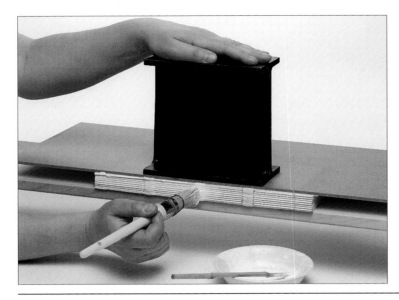

3 Cover the block with a piece of cardboard and place a weight on top. Using the round brush, spread a generous coat of glue along the whole spine. Allow it to dry briefly and in the meantime, prepare the mull to be glued onto the spine.

4 Cut the mull (without paper), making it 1½-inches wider than the spine, and the same height as the book. Place it on a wooden board and coat it with glue.

5 When the glue has been put on the paperless mull, the latter becomes softer. Therefore, transfer it from the board, where you glued it to a clean surface, and let it dry for a few seconds.

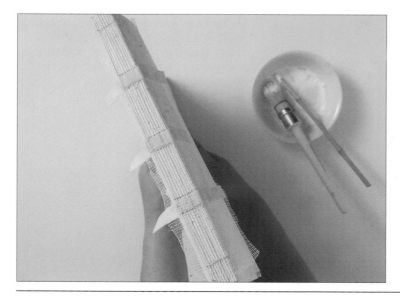

6 Attach the mull to the spine—it must protrude ¾ inch per side—and make it adhere, using the scrubbing brush to help you.

7 Cut the headband and glue it to the two ends of the spine. Slip a sheet of waste paper between the flyleaves (first at the head and then at the tail). Spread the glue and attach the book block to the cover.

8 Close the book and check that the book block is properly placed inside the cover.

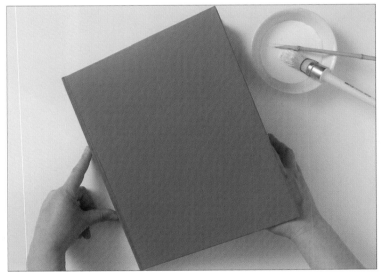

9 Open the cover. Pass a clean cloth over the flyleaf surfaces to flatten them well. Your book is now ready for its place on your bookshelves.

BINDING A NOTEBOOK ON A HOMEMADE SEWING FRAME

This notebook, which uses quality paper for both the pages and the cover, can be created on a homemade sewing frame.

CHARACTERISTICS

– *bookbinding with a stool*
– *flyleaves with flaps*
– *finished format 5 x 7 inches*
– *full-stitching on two hemp twines*

Difficulty: medium
Time: 3–4 hours

REQUIREMENTS

TOOLS
A STOOL
SCISSORS
SAW
A FLAT AND A ROUND PASTE
BRUSH
UNRAVELLING BOARD
NEEDLE

MATERIALS
20 SHEETS OF FABRIANO 5 ART
PAPER, 130 GRAMS, FORMAT
$19^3/_4 \times 27^1/_2$ INCHES
1 SHEET OF GLOSSY EMBOSSED
PAPER
HEMP TWINE
20 INCHES OF MULL
YARN, NUMBER 25
$1/_8$-INCH THICK CARDBOARD

FROM SEWING TO THE COVER

1 Begin by folding the sheets in groups of five. Take two sheets for the flyleaves and fold them in half.

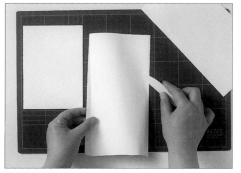

2 Cut them the same height as the book, but add 1/2 inch more for the width. Insert the notebook into the book press. Mark on the spine the slots that will be sawed. Saw the slots with only one movement.

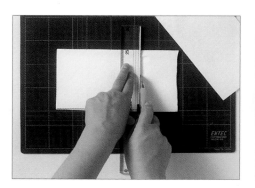

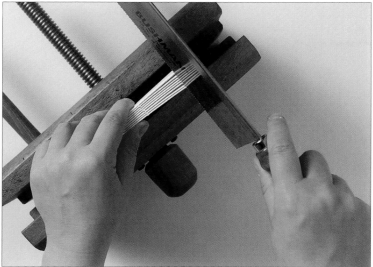

3 Along the fold of the flyleaves, make a line 1/2 inch from the spine. Fold it with the bone folder. Spread a coat of glue onto the two inner parts of the fold and place a signature there. Press with the bone folder to make it stick. Repeat these steps with the end flyleaves.

4 Take the stool and turn it upside down. Cut a piece of cardboard that fits exactly between the four legs—it will act as a work board. You could also use a wooden table.

5 Cut off the two front corners of the cardboard so that it is exactly aligned with the hemp twines when they are positioned. Tie the first twine to the base of the stool and attach it to the top.

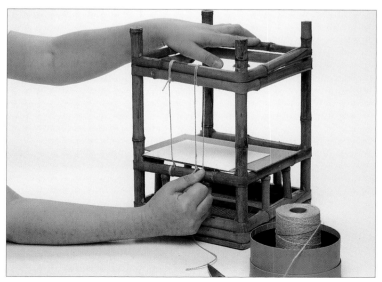

6 Proceed in the same way for the second twine. Prepare the proper length of thread, thread the needle, and enter the first hole, thus beginning the sewing operation like the previous projects.

7 Be careful when sewing the first three or four signatures, as it will be a little more difficult to keep them steady and aligned. When each signature has been sewn, remember to do the link-stitch at both ends.

8 When the last signature has been sewn, make a double knot and cut the thread. Cut the twines as well, leaving strips about 2-inches long.

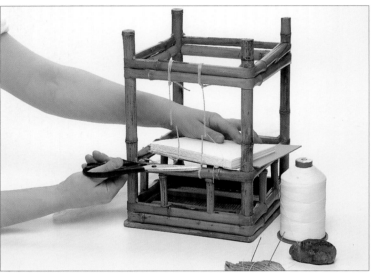

9 Now start preparing for the book block. Unravel the twines, glue them to the flyleaf (laying them out with the bone folder), and coat the spine with glue. Let it dry. Cut out a strip of mull, spread glue on it, and let it dry for a few seconds. Then, attach it evenly along the spine of the notebook.

10 Shorten the sheet of the first flyleaf to obtain a flap. Cut off the two corners with scissors and get ready to work on the cover.

11 With the utility knife, cut out from the cardboard the two rectangles for the cover and the central spine. Mark the measurements on the back of the lining paper, remembering to mark also the two side grooves. When cutting, remember to keep the extra amount necessary for the turn-ins. Coat the sheet with glue, let it dry for a few seconds, and then position the cover boards and spine along the traced lines.

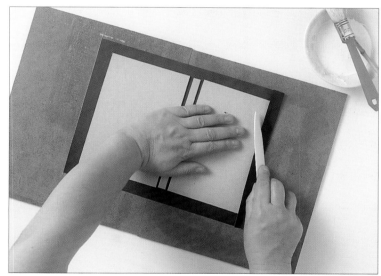

12 To case the notebook, proceed like the previous projects. Close the book, wait for it to dry, and then open it.
The notebook is now ready to become a very unique gift.

BINDING WITHOUT A SEWING FRAME

BINDING WITH NAILS

The two projects shown in this chapter include techniques that do not require a sewing frame.
You will find them useful for binding volumes of loose sheets.

CHARACTERISTICS

– binding with nails
– full cloth cover
– flyleaves reinforced with
  strips of cardboard

Difficulty: minimum
Time: 3–4 hours

REQUIREMENTS

TOOLS
HAMMER
FLAT-HEADED NAILS FOR WOOD
($1/_2$-INCH LONG)
SCISSORS
WEIGHTS
UTILITY KNIFE
FLAT PASTE BRUSH

MATERIALS
250 WHITE SHEETS, 70 GRAMS,
FORMAT 8 $1/_3$ X 11$1/_2$ INCHES
$1/_8$-INCH THICK CARDBOARD
$1/_{16}$-INCH THICK CARD FOR SPINE
BACKING
MULL
WHITE (PVA) GLUE
1$1/_8$ YARDS OF COLORED
BOOKBINDER'S CLOTH
1 SHEET, 27$1/_2$ X 39$1/_2$ INCHES,
130 GRAMS FOR THE FLYLEAVES

FROM ALIGNING TO THE COVER

1 Take the ream of loose sheets and align them like the previous projects. Then, arch it and straighten it once more, holding the first sheet with your thumbs.

2 Let air circulate among the sheets, let go of your grasp, and place the sheets on your workspace. Be sure to keep them in a vertical position and slightly concave to prevent them from slipping.

3 Continue to hold them vertical to the workspace. Gather them once again to remake the ream. Tap them lightly on the table and they should slide by themselves. Align them and keep them compact.

4 Lay the ream on your workspace. Hold it steady with one hand and, with the other, eliminate any air that may have remained between the sheets.

5 Place the ream under weights to align the sheets exactly. In the meantime, prepare the flyleaves. Cut two sheets that are twice the format of the book. Fold them in half. Crease the fold well with the bone folder.

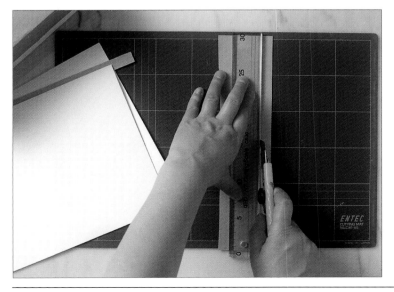

6 With the utility knife and the ruler, cut two strips from the cardboard as high as the book and $5/8$-inch wide. They must be precisely cut.

7 Coat the two strips of cardboard with glue, wait a few seconds, and then position them on the edge of each flyleaf fold. Press to make them adhere well.

8 Grasp the ream of sheets firmly and place them within the two flyleaves you have just made.

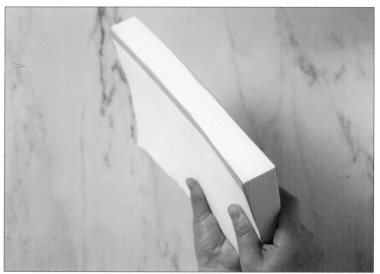

9 Align the stack of sheets perfectly once more and, being careful to keep it aligned, put it under the weight. Keep the weight a short distance from the edge.

10 Take the hammer and nail the first nail exactly into the center of the cardboard strip. Nail the others at a distance of 1 inch. Turn the volume over and attach the nails at alternative distances from those of the opposite side.

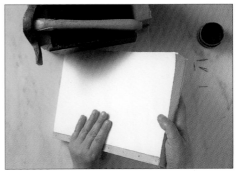

11 When the book block has been nailed, you can handle it without fear. Cut out the two cover boards from the cardboard—measurement starts from the inside of the cardboard strip that is glued onto the flyleaves. Measure the spine and cut it out.

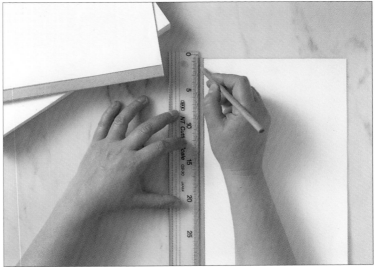

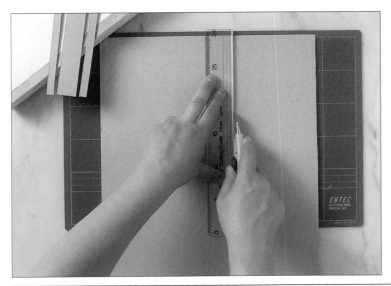

12 Unlike the covers made up to now, for this one you must also cut two cardboard strips $1/2$-inch wide. They will be attached between the spine and the cover boards.

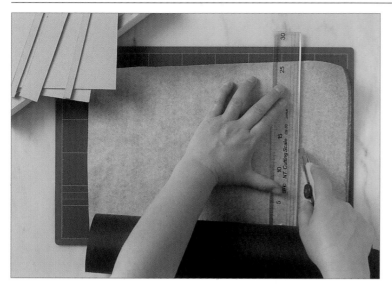

13 Start cutting the cloth, taking into consideration the size of the spine, the two side strips, the two cover boards, and the extra amount needed for the turn-ins (at least $^3/_4$ inch per side).

14 To make it easier for you and to prevent mistakes, place all the pieces of the cover onto the cut cloth. With the pieces and the ruler, mark out the outlines: spine in the center, groove $^1/_4$ inch away, strip of cardboard $^1/_2$-inch wide, groove $^1/_4$ inch away, width of the cardboard cover board, and turn-in.

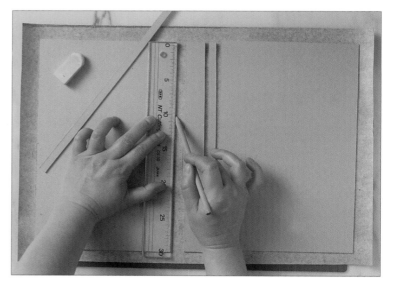

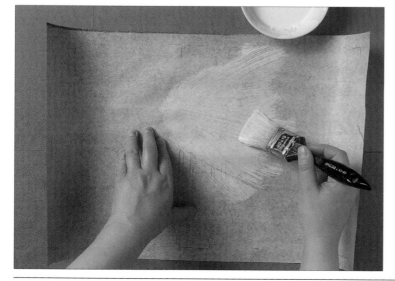

15 Lay the cloth out on a clean workspace and, holding it steady with one hand, spread it with glue, using quick, "bicycle spoke" movements.

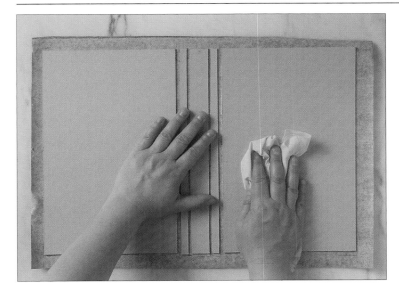

16 Lift the cloth with the bone folder tip and lay it out on a clean space. Wait a few seconds. Then, begin to position it. If you follow the outlines on the cloth, you will have no difficulty in arranging all the pieces and making them adhere to the cloth. Press with a soft cloth.

17 When all the sides have been turned in, enforce the grooves with the bone folder and close the cover. Make sure that the ends are perfectly aligned.

18 Case the book block into the cover. Place a sheet of waste paper between the flyleaf and the first page and glue. Let dry. Throw away the waste paper and repeat the operation for the end of the book.

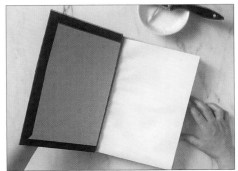

A SEWN NOTEBOOK

This project will allow you to make a notebook in a hurry. You can use it for your home notes, memories, or favorite recipes. The quick and easy sewing technique used is called "tie-stitch", and is ideal for sewing together cards.

CHARACTERISTICS
– tie-stitch sewing

Difficulty: medium
Time: 4 hours

REQUIREMENTS

TOOLS

NEEDLE
AWL
UTILITY KNIFE
SCISSORS
RULER
FLAT BONE FOLDER
PASTE BRUSH
PENCIL
RUBBER

MATERIALS

2 SHEETS OF STRAW BOARD,
FORMAT $19^3/_4$ X $27^1/_2$ INCHES
WHITE SHEETS, 60 GRAMS,
FORMAT $12^1/_2$ X $8^1/_4$ INCHES
BOOKBINDER'S GLUE
THREAD, NUMBER 0

FROM FOLDING TO THE SEWN NOTEBOOK

1 Fold three small signatures (each signature consisting of five sheets) in half. You will now have thirty folded sheets measuring $16^{1}/_{4}$ x $8^{1}/_{4}$ inches.

2 For the cover, take a sheet of straw board. Fold it in half. You will now have a sheet 10-inches high and $27^{1}/_{2}$-inches wide. Fold it in half along its width and cut it 3-inches wider than the notebook. Open it and groove at the center with the bone folder.

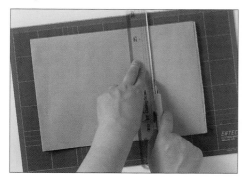

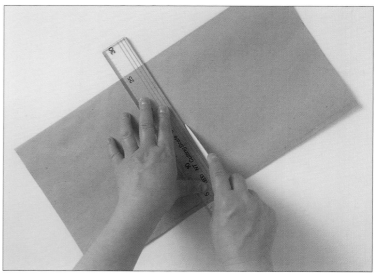

3 Fold it once more in half. You now will have a 10 x 14-inches double sheet, which is not folded on its lower side. Open it and lay an open signature on it. Measure so that the cover is $^{1}/_{4}$-inch higher at the head and $^{1}/_{4}$ inch at the tail. Cut them.

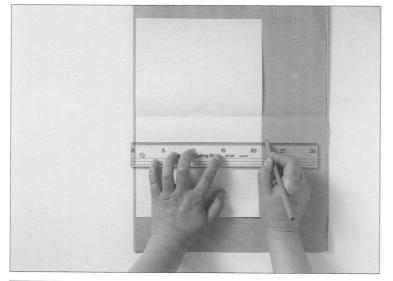

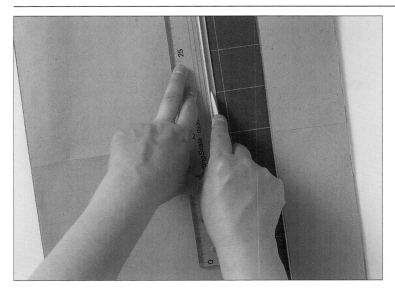

4 Make a groove with the bone folder at a distance of ¼ inch. Take a piece of card and from the lower part, where the sheets are not folded double, spread the glue ¼ inch from the edge and turn in (put a coat of glue also between the loose leaves).

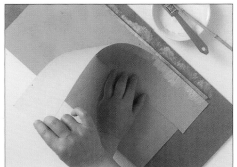

5 You now have a double cover 3¼-inches wider than the sheets. Position the sheets onto the center of the cover and mark three holes with the awl: the first in the center and the other two 2 inches away from the center.

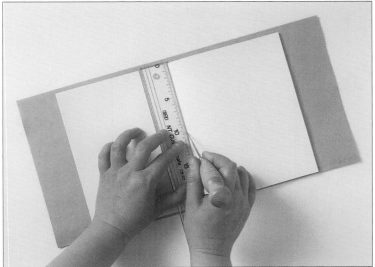

6 Pierce the points where you will sew with the awl. Thread the needle and begin sewing from the hole on your right, entering from the outside towards the inside.

7 Continue sewing, bringing the needle through the central hole from the inside out. Then pass it into the third hole and exit it from the central hole.

8 Take the thread you left at the beginning and tie it to the head of the thread in your needle. Make a tight double knot.

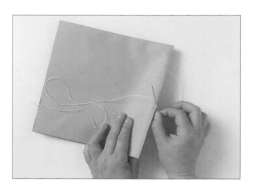

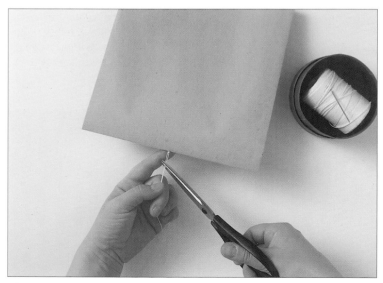

9 Cut the thread and open the notebook. Mark a groove with the tip of the bone folder along both the edge line of the sheets and ¼ inch from the cover edge.

10 These grooves will help you when making subsequent folds. Spread glue on the flap previously marked. Do the same with the other flap.

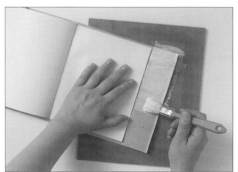

11 Fold the protruding parts of the cover and glue them onto the first and last pages of the notebook. The cover will be strengthened by the glued sheets, which act as flyleaves. Fold the cover, moving it all to the left.

12 Place on the mat the inside of the notebook. Take the ruler and at a distance of $1/4$ inch from the edge, trim the inside of the notebook with the utility knife. It is now ready for use.

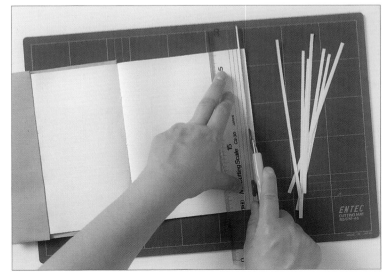

INDEX

A
Accessories, 34–35
Adhesives
    natural, 43
    synthetic, 43
Aligning the paper, 39, 54–57, 92
Art paper, 20
Aspect, of paper, 18

B
Back, 12
Backing, 12
Backlining, 12
Bands, 12
Binding, 12
    by sewing on tape.
        See Sewing on tape
    with sewing frame.
        See Projects
    without sewing frame, 141–159
Boards, 12
Book block, 12
    cloth for, 32
    making, 69–74, 98–101
    positioning, 85
Book press, 30
Bookmark, 12
Brief drying, 12
Bristol, 16

C
Calico, 32
Cardboard, 16–17
    cutting, 76–77
    grain of, 38
Case cover
    cardboard, cutting, 76–77
    casing, 86–87
    cloth, cutting, 77
    gluing the cloth, 79–85
    measuring the cover, 76
    paper, cutting, 78–79
    positioning the book block, 85
    making, 102–105
    with cloth corners, 75–87
Casing, 12, 86–87
Cloth
    cutting, 77
    for book block preparation, 32
    for covers, 28
    gluing, 79–85
Cloth cover, 117–119
Colophon, 12
Cordonnet, 32
Corners, 12
Counting
    fanned sheets, 41
    the sections, 92
    the sheets, 40
Cover, 12, 13
    cloth, making of, 117–119
    cloth for, 28
    industrial paper for, 24
    measuring, 76
Cover boards, 12, 13
Covering, 12
Creasing, 12

Cutting
    cardboard, 76–77
    cloth, 77
    paper, 78–79

E
Edge, 12, 13

F
Fabriano papers, for inside
    pages, 20
Flaps, 12
Flyleaves, 12–13, 46
    double, 93–95
    German-style folded, 46–47
    glued, 46, 60–61
    paper for, 22
Folding the sheets, 42
Fore-edge, 13
Full-stitch sewing, 45

G
Gap, 13
Glossary, 12–13
Glue, 43
Gluing, 99
    cloth, 79–85
    direct, 43
    half cloth and paper journal,
        71–74
    ribbon, 43
Grain
    of cardboard, 38
    of paper, 38
Grey board, 16
"Grifo" laid paper, 20
Groove, 13

H
Half cloth and paper journal
    making the book block, 69–74
    preparations for sewing, 53–61
    sewing, 64–68
    sewing frame preparation,
        63–64
    with rounded spine. *See* Half
        cloth and paper journal with
        rounded spine
Half cloth and paper journal
    with rounded spine, 88–101
    making the book block,
        98–101
    preparation for sewing, 91–96
    requirements, 90
    sewing, 96–97
Half-stitch sewing, 45
Head, 13
Headband, 13, 32
Hemp twine, 32
Historical outline, 8–11

I
Industrial paper, for covers, 24
"Ingres" paper, 22

L
Link-stitch sewing, 44

M
Machine made
    cardboard, 16
    paper, 18
Materials, 15–35
    book press, 30
    cardboard, 16–17
    cloth for covers, 28
    for sewing with sewing frame,
        32
    paper, 18–27
    sewing frame, 30–31
    tools/accessories, 34–35
Measuring, cover, 76
Mill board, 16
Mull, 32

N
Nails, binding with, 143–151
    aligning the sheets, 146–147
    cutting cardboard, 147
    making the book block,
        148–151
    requirements, 144
Notebook
    binding on homemade sewing
        frame, 132–139
    characteristics, 133
    from sewing to the cover,
        135–139
    requirements, 134
    sewn. *See* Sewn notebook

P
Paper, 18–28
    aligning, 39, 54–57, 92
    counting fanned sheets, 41
    counting the sheets, 40
    cutting, 78–79
    folding the sheets, 42
    for flyleaves, 22
    for inside pages, 20
    grain of, 38
    handmade, 26
    industrial, for covers, 24
    machine made, 18
    painted, 26
    special characteristics, 18
Positioning, the book block, 85
Projects, 49–134
    case cover, 102–105
    case cover with cloth corners,
        75–87
    cloth cover, 117–119
    half cloth and paper journal,
        50–87
    half cloth and paper journal
        with rounded spine, 88–101
    notebook on homemade
        publications, binding into
        book, 106–116
    sewing frame, 132–139
    sewing on tape, 120–131
    without sewing frame, 141–159
Publications, binding into books,
    106–116
    characteristics, 107

    method, 110–116
    requirements, 108

R
Rattle, 18
Ribbon, 32, 43
"Roma" paper, 20
Rounding, 13, 100–101, 104–105
Rules, basic, 37–47

S
Sawing, 44, 58–60, 95–96
Scrubbing brush, 13
Sewing, 13, 44–45
    full-stitch, 45
    half cloth and paper journal,
        64–68
    half cloth and paper journal
        with rounded spine, 96–97
    half-stitch, 45
    link-stitch, 44
Sewing frame, 30–31
    binding projects. *See* Projects
    homemade, 133, 137–138
    preparation, 63–64
    sewing materials for, 32
Sewing on tape
    characteristics, 121
    method, 123–131
    requirements, 122
Sewn notebook, 152–159
    characteristics, 153
    folding the paper, 156–157
    preparation for sewing, 157
    requirements, 154
    sewing, 158–159
Shoulder, 13
Signature or section, 13
Spine, 13
    rounding, 100–101, 104–105
Split nuts, 13
Square (projecting edge), 13
Straw board, 16
Surfaces, 13

T
Tail, 13
Tape, 32
Tapping, 13. *See also* Aligning
    the paper
Thickness, of paper, 18
Thread, 32
Tightening the twines, 70–71, 99
Title page, 13
Tools, 34–35
Trimming, 13
Turn-ins, 13
Twines, tightening, 70–71, 99

V
"Vergatona" paper, 20

W
Waste paper, 13
Weight, of paper, 18